"I AM A REALIST IN ALL
ASPECTS OF LIFE. I REFUSE
TO ACCEPT SOCIETY'S SET OF
STANDARDS, OR MORALITY.
AS A ONE PERCENTER, WE
BUILD A WORLD OF OUR OWN
THAT VERY FEW CAN GRASP."

—BREEZE, ONE PERCENTER

RIDING FREE IN THE 21ST CENTURY

PERCENTER REVOLUTION

DAVE NICHOLS

♠

m motorbooks

Quarto is the authority on a wide range of topics.

Quarto educates, entertains and enriches the lives of
our readers—enthusiasts and lovers of hands-on living.

www.quartoknows.com

First published in 2017 by Motorbooks, an imprint of Quarto Publishing Group USA Inc.,
400 First Avenue North, Suite 400, Minneapolis, MN 55401 USA.

Telephone: (612) 344-8100 Fax: (612) 344-8692
quartoknows.com
Visit our blogs at quartoknows.com

10 9 8 7 6 5 4 3 2 1

ISBN: 978-0-7603-5238-0

Library of Congress Cataloging-in-Publication Data

Names: Nichols, Dave, 1954- author.
Title: One percenter revolution : riding free in the 21st century / Dave Nichols.
Description: Minneapolis, Minnesota : Motorbooks, an imprint of Quarto
    Publishing Group USA Inc., [2017] | Includes index.
Identifiers: LCCN 2016041494 | ISBN 9780760352380 (hc w/jacket)
Subjects: LCSH: Motorcycle gangs--United States. | Motorcycle clubs--United
    States. | Motorcycling--Social aspects--United States.
Classification: LCC HV6439.U5 N54 2017 | DDC 364.106/60973--dc23
LC record available at https://lccn.loc.gov/2016041494

Acquiring Editor: Darwin Holmstrom
Creative Director: Laura Drew
Project Manager: Jordan Wiklund
Art Director: Cindy Samargia Laun
Cover Illustration and Design: Ryan Quickfall
Book Design and Layout: Silverglass Design

On the back cover: Knees in the breeze, Ben Zales kicks back on his chopper as he enters
    Joshua Tree National Park on Nash's Hell Ride.
On the endpapers: Ripping around downtown with a hitchhiker on the cobra seat (front).
    Jeff and his long Knucklehead chopper are livin' the dream, overlooking the Pacific Ocean
    in Malibu, California (back).

Printed in China

CONTENTS

"THE PERFECT MAN? A POET ON A MOTORCYCLE."
—LUCINDA WILLIAMS, SINGER, SONGWRITER

INTROD

UCTION

FORWARD: INTO THE PAST!

One percenter motorcycle clubs are made up of men who do not compromise their values or code of honor. In a nation of sheep, they are wolves. Known to be fiercely loyal to their club brothers, one percenters are members of a tribe that is not to be trifled with. They are the modern-day equivalent of such rebellious spirits as Mongols, Huns, Vikings, pirates, and gunslingers.

Andre rides easy through Death Valley on his Panhead chopper. To today's chopper riders, everything old is cool again.

"WE WANT TO BE FREE TO RIDE OUR MACHINES WITHOUT BEING HASSLED BY THE MAN! AND WE WANT TO GET LOADED. AND WE WANT TO HAVE A GOOD TIME. AND THAT'S WHAT WE'RE GONNA DO!"

—PETER FONDA AS HEAVENLY BLUES IN *WILD ANGELS*

This is the third book in a trilogy that delves into the outlaw biker lifestyle and one percenter motorcycle clubs. We explored the long history of rebellion in *One Percenter: The Legend of the Outlaw Biker* and discovered that there is a very real need for those rare rebel breeds of humans who dare to venture off any known map to discover what lies beyond. Rebels stir the bubbling caldron of society and add freethinking pepper and spice to conventional thought. The second book, *The One Percenter Code: How to Be An Outlaw in a World Gone Soft*, examines the creation of a strict code of honor for the warrior class known as the modern biker.

As the original post–World War II wild ones of the 1940s and '50s became grandpas and then great-grandpas, a new generation

BELOW: View from the handlebars, riding into downtown Los Angeles. OPPOSITE: Gentry kicking over his Knucklehead at California's Born Free, the largest next-gen bike show in America today.

Tony and his Ironhead
chop job in Lake Tahoe.

"I BELONGED RIGHT WHERE I WAS, WITH MY CLUB. I DIDN'T HAVE MILLIONS OF DOLLARS AND WASN'T ON THE COVER OF *TIME* MAGAZINE EITHER, BUT WHAT I DID HAVE WAS RESPECT. RESPECT FROM THOSE WHO COUNTED ON ME. AFTER ALL, I SAID TO MYSELF, I WAS SONNY BARGER. I WAS A HELLS ANGEL."

—SONNY BARGER, HELLS ANGEL

of outlaw biker emerged on the American scene. Many were the sons of the originals, who followed in their fathers' engineer boots. Others felt a sense of brotherhood found in the clubs, witnessed in biker movies and magazines, and entered this biker lifestyle. These free spirits exist to push the envelope of convention and twist the grip of their loud motorcycles. They just like to shake things up!

In 2008, an interesting thing happened: TV producer Kurt Sutter's crime drama *Sons of Anarchy* hit the FX Channel and excited viewers everywhere got a glimpse inside a fictitious one percenter motorcycle club. The series ran for seven seasons and was the highest rated show on cable television. Families who were once terrified by bikers found them to be fascinating and fun to watch. At our coast-to-coast Easyriders Custom Bike Shows, real one percenters mix with motorcycle-riding hobbyists and plain folks. Little kids would smile and wave at these modern-day Vikings; parents would encourage photo ops, never realizing that what they were proposing was much like having their precious little ones take a selfie with a grizzly bear. One percenter bikers suddenly seemed to be tamed and docile, like tigers at the zoo seen behind thick glass.

Inspired by *Sons of Anarchy,* twenty-something bikers, low on dough but high on riding stripped-down murdercycles, flipped the finger to the straight world just as generations before them have done. While roaring off to the sound of an entirely new drummer, today's latest breed of biker is often a mix of a brilliant mind, a warped sense of humor, a love of old iron, and an abiding respect for the hardcore one percenters who have ridden the trail before him. This book is dedicated to this new breed of rebel rousers and highway hooligans, the true authors of the one percenter revolution.

—DAVE NICHOLS

1

A NEW GENERATION OF REBEL

♠

On January 9 and 10, 2016, many thousands of custom motorcycle enthusiasts poured into the Sacramento Convention Center for the Easyriders Bike Show. The tour of five shows across the country is heralded as "The hottest custom motorcycle shows in America." As editor-in-chief of *Easyriders* magazine, the biker's bible for over forty-five years, I have had the honor and privilege of judging the bike shows for more than twenty years. Every January and February I find myself in gigantic convention centers in Long Beach, Sacramento, Charlotte, Nashville, and at our big Invitational Bike Show blowout in Columbus. Me and the other editors of our Paisano Publications stable of motorcycle magazines find the very latest, freshest, and most innovative custom bikes by the country's top builders at these shows. Besides offering our readers a way to stay connected with the biker world during the winter months, these shows offer a way to find truly great custom motorcycles to photograph for features in our publications.

OPPOSITE: This racer proves not all cool Harleys are choppers as he pushes his Tracker Sportster into the 1 Moto Show in Portland, Oregon.

Many years ago, these bike shows mainly attracted the more hardcore, dedicated crowds of motorcycle enthusiasts, but since the arrival of reality TV shows that featured custom bike builders as wrench-wielding stars back in 2000 or so, we have seen our audience change to include a more mainstream crowd and a lot of families. In fact, we have even had to rent strollers to the public in order to keep up with family-oriented motorcycle fans at our bike shows.

Each year since the inception of the TV series *Sons of Anarchy*, the Easyriders Bike Show Tour has featured many of the show's stars. Over the years, event-goers could stand in line for autographs and photo ops with series regulars Charlie Hunnam, Theo Rossi, Tommy Flanagan, Mark "Bobby" Boone, Ryan "Opie" Hurst and, for the 2016 Tour, Rusty "Quinn" Coones. At six-foot, six-inches and 285 bodybuilding pounds, Rusty is a mild-mannered giant Viking of a man. Known foremost for his bike-building prowess in southern California, Rusty actually built

The TV series that made hardcore one percenters everybody's new best friends. The FX Network hit *Sons of Anarchy* aired for six seasons (2008 to 2014) and told the story of a fictitious motorcycle club in California. The show's creator Kurt Sutter says he based the series on *Hamlet*. Kids all over the country were dressing like one percenters and wearing *SOA* T-shirts.

and maintained some of the motorcycles used in the TV series. Rusty is also a member of a one percenter motorcycle club.

While *Sons of Anarchy* focuses on a make-believe one percenter club, it is based on very real outlaw motorcycle clubs such as the Hells Angels, the Mongols, the Vagos, the Bandidos, the Sons of Silence, the Outlaws, and the Pagans. While Rusty may be a mild-mannered, gentle giant to his fans and friends, he also lives by the one percenter code and has a lifetime of hard

"BIKE STYLES ARE LIKE LADIES' SKIRT HEMLINES—
THEY'RE UP, THEY'RE DOWN, THEY'RE UP AGAIN.
A CLASSIC CHOPPER IS NEVER OUT OF STYLE AND
LOOKS AS GOOD TODAY AS IT DID FORTY YEARS AGO,
AND IT'LL STILL LOOK GOOD IN ANOTHER TWENTY."

—IRISH RICH

riding brotherhood under his belt. He is the real deal. Although he didn't wear his colors when he represented *Sons of Anarchy* at our Easyriders Bike Shows (like club members who *do* wear their colors when they are seen by the public), he represented his club. He was the club, as were his brothers who attended wearing their colors. None of them wants to reflect poorly on their club. If trouble does raise its head, it is dealt with quickly and efficiently.

Case in point: the Sacramento area is known to be Hells Angels territory and many members of the Red & White attend our show there each year. Various chapters even have booths at the show selling support T-shirts, hats, and the like. Because of this, each year the Sacramento Police Department and members of the Bureau of Alcohol, Tobacco and Firearms send undercover cops and agents to our Sacramento Bike Show to keep an eye on anyone wearing a motorcycle club patch on their backs.

From a long room, high above the convention center floor, these police officers and agents squint through high-tech cameras and record endless images of every one percenter in the building. While the cops keep this surveillance low key, every club member in the building knows that they are being watched, identified, and scrutinized. Down on the show floor, uniformed police stroll about to offer a visual presence while plainclothes cops look at the bikes on display and keep an eye on all the motorcycle club members.

In 2015 I was up in the surveillance room, which the editors also use as our judging room, and was looking down through the shuttered glass windows when a small skirmish broke out. It seemed that a member of one outlaw club had a problem with a member of another club. Someone looked at a patch-holder the wrong way or said the wrong thing. Then chests got pumped up and someone got into someone else's face. I won't call this a fight because the whole thing from beginning to end only took place over a few seconds. The two one percenters squared off, someone pushed someone, and the police

"IT TAKES MORE THAN GOING DOWN TO THE VIDEO STORE AND RENTING EASY RIDER TO BE A REBEL."

—DENNIS HOPPER

swarmed on the two men and took them outside. This happened so quickly that the packed crowds of families standing a few feet away never saw a thing. There was just one tiny problem: one of the two bikers dropped a gun on the concrete floor. The police instantly scooped up the weapon and the ruckus was over.

Though this was a fairly lackluster happening in an otherwise completely safe and peaceful event, it caused the local police to change their tactics for our 2016 show. During the 2016 Sacramento Bike Show, the police took over the entire upstairs rooms for their stepped up surveillance of all one percenter clubs and demanded special video cameras throughout the hall. They added more uniformed and undercover cops to patrol the event and also set up metal detectors at the entrances where everyone entering the facility was frisked and patted down for weapons.

While the general public perceives outlaw bikers as photo opportunities for their kids, just like the grizzly bears national park visitors pose with for selfies, real one percenters are far from toothless, clawless tigers who are strutted out for your amusement. Though they have learned to tone it down for the press and the public, outlaw bikers are still the real deal and should always be treated with respect. Though long in the tooth, old-school, hardcore bikers' fangs are still plenty sharp.

In order to understand how the public developed this perception of one percenters as pussycats, we must journey back in time to appreciate the origination of this pasteurization process.

THE ORIGINAL WILD ONES

The first real outlaw motorcycle clubs were populated by men who had come back from World War II with a need for speed they could only satisfy aboard stripped-down motorcycles. The men who started such motorcycle clubs as the Boozerfighters, 13 Rebels, the Galloping Gooses, and Yellow Jackets had much in common with servicemen returning from war today. Then and now, they are often disillusioned souls who no longer feel they fit into society and are more at home on the saddles of their motorcycles and in the brotherhood found in motorcycle clubs.

We have the media to thank for the exaggerated view that motorcyclists are modern-day Huns on wheels, out to take over your town and destroy your red, white, and blue way of life. There's no doubt that the image of the leather-clad hellion blasting down the road on a loud Harley comes from some mildly anti-social activities that took place at an AMA Gypsy Tour on July 4, 1947, in Hollister, California. Much has been written about this "occurrence," though little that the media of the day reported on regarding what they called "the Hollister Riot" was actually true.

The city fathers in Hollister had put on motorcycle races long before the alleged riot and never had any problems with rowdy riders.

Out of the nearly three thousand riders who came to watch the races and be part of the Hollister rally, the riders who were members of clubs not sanctioned by the American

ABOVE: One of the most iconic biker-related photos ever taken. Marlon Brando played Johnny Strabler in the 1953 Stanley Kramer film *The Wild One*. While most of Johnny's Black Rebels Motorcycle Club rode Harleys, Brando roared around on a Triumph Thunderbird. RIGHT: *The Wild One* was based loosely on the 1947 Hollister Riot as told by Frank Rooney's short story "The Cyclists' Raid," originally published by *Harper's* magazine.

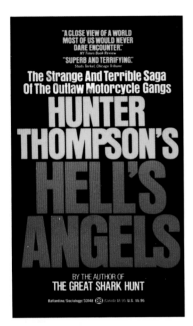

"A CLOSE VIEW OF A WORLD
MOST OF US WOULD NEVER
DARE ENCOUNTER."
NY Times Book Review

"SUPERB AND TERRIFYING."
Studs Terkel, Chicago Tribune

**The Strange And Terrible Saga
Of The Outlaw Motorcycle Gangs**

**HUNTER
THOMPSON'S
HELL'S
ANGELS**

BY THE AUTHOR OF
THE GREAT SHARK HUNT

Ballantine/Sociology/33148 🐐 /Canada $6.95/ U.S. $5.95

Gonzo journalist Hunter S. Thompson
managed to spend a lot of time with the
Oakland Chapter of the Hells Angels to
research his ground-breaking book that
was published in 1966. *The New York Times*
described Thompson's portrayal as, "a world
most of us would never dare encounter."

Motorcycle Association only amounted to a handful. The
misdemeanors that supposedly took place over the course
of the weekend were pretty much of the public-intoxication
or drunk-and-disorderly variety. For example, one guy
was cited for trying to urinate into the radiator of his truck.
There was racing in the streets, whooping, hollering, and
plenty of drinking, but not anything more outrageous than
you'd find at a college frat party. About the worst thing
that happened was that somebody stole a cop's hat.

To sell newspapers, the *San Francisco Chronicle*
exaggerated the event, and a magazine article in the July
1947 issue of *Life* turned this supposed "riot" into the
stuff of legend, giving birth to the concept of the outlaw
biker. Writer Frank Rooney created an overblown fictional
takeoff based loosely on the Hollister Riot, called *Cycle
Raid*, that was printed in *Harper's* magazine in 1951, further
hyperbolizing the image of the outlaw motorcyclist.

Always ready to cash in on a trend, Hollywood
moviemakers capitalized on this incredible new black
leather-clad villain. Producer Stanley Kramer used
Rooney's fictional account of motorized mayhem along
with the events at Hollister as the basis for his 1954 film *The Wild One*, starring
Marlon Brando and Lee Marvin. The film spawned an entire genre—the biker
film—which in turn became a self-fulfilling prophecy. In the ensuing years,
motorcycle clubs around the world based themselves on the fictitious biker
codes of conduct found in the images presented in American biker films.

The Hollister Riot gave rise to the very term "one percenter." After the
Gypsy Tour Races in Hollister generated negative publicity for one of its
events, the AMA issued a press release explaining that the "rough" element
of the motorcycling public amounted to only "one percent" of the total riding
community. They proclaimed that the vast majority of motorcyclists were
good, clean Americans with jobs and families. Naturally, outlaw clubs that
were sprouting up across the country liked the idea of being the one percent
that your momma warned you about and the term "one percenter" was born. It

LEFT: Peter Fonda (standing) played Heavenly Blues in the 1966 biker flick *The Wild Angels*. In the movie's climatic orgy in a small town church, Fonda delivers his classic dialog regarding, "We want to be free! We want to be free to do what we wanna do! We wanna be free to ride our machines without being hassled by the man! And we wanna get loaded! And we wanna have a good time!" BELOW: The Roger Corman biker flick came out before *Easy Rider*, and besides Peter Fonda, Nancy Sinatra, Bruce Dern, and Diane Ladd, it featured actual members of the Hells Angels who basically worked for beer and pot.

Their credo is violence... Their God is hate... and they call themselves

THE WILD ANGELS'

AMERICAN INTERNATIONAL presents
PETER FONDA NANCY SINATRA

THE WILD ANGELS
PANAVISION® & PATHECOLOR

CO-STARRING BRUCE DERN and DIANE LADD

ROGER CORMAN
CHARLES GRIFFITH

MEMBERS OF HELL'S ANGELS
OF VENICE, CALIFORNIA

wasn't long before a diamond-shaped patch began to appear on cut-off denims and leathers. The diamond one percenter patch was—and is—a badge of honor to those outsiders spurned by society.

HELL ON WHEELS

Over the next twenty years, one percenter motorcycle clubs took on a darker hue. Gone from the media focus were the "drinking clubs with motorcycle problems" such as the Boozerfighters, because we were told that the Hells Angels were burning into town to rape your daughters. This had to do with an incident that occurred during Labor Day weekend back in 1964.

Hells Angels and other one percenter clubs were having a run up to Monterey, California, to raise funds to send a fallen brother's body home for

'BLACK SOULS'
vs.
THE 'STOMPERS'
...in the
DEADLIEST
CYCLE WAR
ever
waged!

DENNIS HOPPER · JODY McCREA · CHRIS NOEL · JOCK MAHONEY
STARRING IN
THE GLORY STOMPERS

The Glory Stompers 1967 #336 **R**

Dennis Hopper heads the cast as the leader of the Black Souls Motorcycle Club, which are at war with another club called the Glory Stompers. This 1967 film by Anthony M. Lanza was typical of the drive-in fodder of the time.

THEY
LAID WASTE
TO THE
FLESH AND
BLOOD OF
AMERICA'S
DAUGHTERS

Their creed:
"If it feels good, do it!"

CAMERON MITCHELL

HOT STEEL BETWEEN THEIR LEGS...
THE WILDEST BUNCH OF THE 70's!

ROARING THROUGH THE STREETS
ON CHOPPED DOWN HOGS!

They steal women...
initiate them into the
pack...sell them
on the black
market of crime!

THE
CYCLE SAVAGES

BRUCE DERN · CHRIS ROBINSON
MELODY PATTERSON
BILL BRAME · MAURICE SMITH
MIKE CURB & CASEY KASEM

FAR LEFT: Hot on the heels of *The Wild Angels*, Bruce Dern and Diane Ladd teamed up with Jack Nicholson, Cameron Mitchell, and Harry Dean Stanton in *Rebel Rousers*. The 1967 film *Rebel Rousers'* plot revolves around what happens when a rebellious biker holds a drag race to determine who will "win" a pregnant girlfriend. LEFT: An even simpler plot is seen in *The Cycle Savages*, in which Bruce Dern hunts down a photographer who took nude photos of his girlfriend. I kid you not, that's the plot. This low-budget wonder was produced by none other than Casey Kasem of American Top 40 fame.

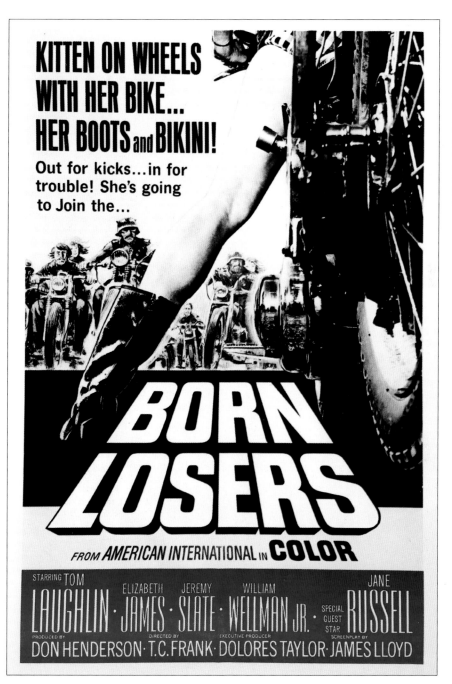

KITTEN ON WHEELS
WITH HER BIKE...
HER BOOTS and BIKINI!

Out for kicks...in for
trouble! She's going
to Join the...

**BORN
LOSERS**

FROM *AMERICAN INTERNATIONAL* IN **COLOR**

STARRING TOM
LAUGHLIN · ELIZABETH JAMES · JEREMY SLATE · WILLIAM WELLMAN JR. · SPECIAL GUEST STAR JANE RUSSELL

PRODUCED BY DON HENDERSON · DIRECTED BY T.C. FRANK · EXECUTIVE PRODUCER DOLORES TAYLOR · SCREENPLAY BY JAMES LLOYD

The Born Losers introduced the world to actor/director Tom Laughlin's character Billy Jack, a Vietnam vet and martial arts pro. A biker club terrorizes a town and rapes some teenaged girls, sending Billy Jack on a tirade where he takes on the club single-handedly.

RIGHT: Peter Fonda starred and produced *Easy Rider* in 1969 along with co-star and the film's director Dennis Hopper. Seated behind Fonda on the Captain America Panhead chopper is none other than a young Jack Nicholson. BELOW: "A man went looking for America and couldn't find it anywhere" reads the poster for *Easy Rider*. The film became the anthem for the Woodstock generation, offering the American biker a cautionary tale regarding "selling out." It was also a huge hit at the box office.

A man went looking for America.
And couldn't find it anywhere...

Cannes Film
Festival
WINNER
'Best Film
By a New
Director'

PANDO COMPANY in association with
RAYBERT PRODUCTIONS presents
easy Rider
starring
PETER FONDA · DENNIS HOPPER · JACK NICHOLSON
Written by
PETER FONDA · DENNIS HOPPER · PETER FONDA · WILLIAM HAYWARD
DENNIS HOPPER
TERRY SOUTHERN · BERT SCHNEIDER · COLOR
Released by COLUMBIA PICTURES

burial. Members of the Oakland chapter of the Hells Angels roared up through Monterey, right through the middle of town, and parked at a big tavern known as Nick's. By three in the afternoon, more than fifty bikes were parked out front.

As the story goes, two girls, one pregnant, and their boyfriends were hanging out and drinking with the club. Local police had provided a secluded stretch of beach for the Angels to camp on, and the party eventually moved to the desolate dunes between Monterey Bay and Fort Ord. The cops even posted a guard on the highway to keep the Angels from taking the party back to town.

The so-called "victims" of this encounter later told police that they went to the beach from Nick's because they wanted to see all the cyclists. The two girls and five male friends joined the party around a roaring bonfire. Club members at the scene remember the girls as being wasted when they arrived. Soon the girls asked to get high and walked away from the fire with a few bikers. Apparently, one of the boyfriends got scared and went for the cops.

By early morning, a roadblock sealed the beach and the two women sat in the back of a police car, pointing out which of the bikers present had supposedly raped them. California newspaper headlines blasted the Hells Angels for allegedly gang raping two minors (supposedly fourteen and fifteen years old) repeatedly. What did not make the papers was that medical examiners reported that neither of the girls had actually been raped. Seems like an important omission. Interestingly, the rape case was not initially first-page national news. Journalists at the time were focusing on the national election story. It wasn't until Attorney General Thomas C. Lynch released a fifteen-page report condemning outlaw bikers that the national media picked up the torch.

Within a few months of the incident, major stories by such media giants as *The Saturday Evening Post*, *Time*, *Newsweek,* and *The New York*

TOP: Also known as *Cycle Psycho, Savage Abduction* is a 1973 thriller written and directed by John Lawrence. A businessman hires a hitman to murder his wife. After accomplishing this task, the killer wants more young girls to kill and the husband hires a motorcycle club to kidnap more girls to torture. This iron pony opera is every bit as good as it sounds. RIGHT: *Angel Unchained* had it all——bikers, cowboys on dune buggies, and a worthless plot. Don Stroud plays Angel, who leaves his motorcycle club to join a hippy commune, where he meets free-spirited Merilee played by Tyne Daly. Then raucous dune buggy boys harass the hippies, and commune leader Luke Askew from *Easy Rider* begs Angel for help. That's pretty much it.

"I THINK I SAW MY FIRST CUSTOM MOTORCYCLE IN 1968 WHEN I WAS ELEVEN. THAT WAS IT FOR ME. I STARTED RIDING WHEN I WAS ELEVEN."

–JERRY COVINGTON, MASTER BUILDER

Luke shows us how to make the
scene, riding into Born Free.

"THAT'S ALL THE MOTORCYCLE IS: A SYSTEM OF CONCEPTS WORKED OUT IN STEEL."

—ROBERT M. PIRSIG, *ZEN AND THE ART OF MOTORCYCLE MAINTENANCE*

Times helped to create the image of the Hells Angels and other motorcycle clubs as degenerate monsters on wheels. The HAs went from obscurity to being the major focus of a modern witch-hunt in nothing flat. Suddenly, reporters came out of the woodwork to get an interview with a real Angel.

At about the same time, journalist Hunter S. Thompson was spending a lot of time with the Oakland chapter of the Angels. He would later turn his encounters into an article for *The Nation* (May 17, 1965) called "Motorcycle Gangs: Losers and Outsiders." Thompson chronicled his experiences with the Hells Angels in the now famous book, *Hell's Angels: The Strange and Terrible Saga of the Outlaw Motorcycle Gangs*.

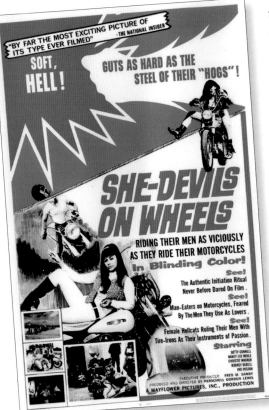

While Thompson's sensationalized book turned more than a few straight stomachs with its look at the raunchy side of the biker lifestyle, the book also paints a picture of the unbridled thrills found when jammin' down the highway on a chopped Harley, inspiring many guys in their teens and twenties to go out a buy a motorcycle. I know it had that effect on me.

Just as with the Hollister incident, the media used the Monterey rape case to sell papers, magazines, and books, making the Hells Angels famous in the process. With fame comes more fame, or infamy,

She-Devils On Wheels stood the biker film genre on its head when Betty Connell played Queen, the leader of an all-girl motorcycle club called the Man-Eaters. This club liked to race each other and then have an orgy at their clubhouse. The race determines the order in which girls pick a man to hump. Unfortunately, new initiate Karen (Christie Wagner) breaks the club's cardinal rule: never fall in love.

Sadly, the 1969 film *Hell's Belles* has nothing to do with female bikers, as the title might imply. Rather, biker Dan, played by Jeremy Slate, gets a motorcycle as a prize after winning a race, but a motorcycle club steals it. Dan has to get his bike back with the help of his girlfriend Cathy, played by Jocelyn Lane.

and it didn't take long for motion picture producers to catch on to the latest exploitable sensation.

The black and white cycle thrills found in *The Wild One* were nothing compared with what was about to come. In 1966, Hunter Thompson's book about the Angels and a picture in *Life* magazine that showed a long line of outlaw bikers attending a biker funeral in California inspired cheap-o horror movie master Roger Corman to get together with veteran screenwriter Charles Griffin and create the screenplay for *The Wild Angels*.

The film's plot, such as it is, follows two members of an outlaw club played by Peter Fonda and Bruce Dern who go in search of a stolen bike. The members

RICHARD K. ROSENBERG in association with RKR ENTERTAINMENT GROUP presents

The True
Story of
an American
Phenomenon.

HELLS ANGELS
FOREVER

Starring THE HELLS ANGELS and Featuring WILLIE NELSON · JERRY GARCIA · JOHNNY PAYCHECK · BO DIDDLEY in
"HELLS ANGELS FOREVER, FOREVER HELLS ANGELS" Original Concept by SANDY ALEXANDER
Written by PETERSON TOOKE and RICHARD CHASE · Narrator MORGAN PAULL · Executive Producers JERRY GARCIA and CLARE FROST
Produced by RICHARD CHASE · SANDY ALEXANDER and LEON GAST · Directed by RICHARD CHASE · KEVIN KEATING and LEON GAST
A BAYLIER FILMS PRODUCTION IN ASSOCIATION WITH WESCOM PRODUCTIONS COLOR Distributed by RKR RELEASING, INC.
R RESTRICTED

Sonny Barger also shows up in the 1983 documentary, *Hell's Angels Forever.* Directors Leon Gast and Richard Chase interview members of the club, who talk about their wild lifestyle and how they are misunderstood by the cops and straight society. Much is revealed about the club's code of honor and love of riding.

"OUR CLUBS AND OUR BIKES ARE WHAT WE LIVE FOR, AND ANYTHING ELSE IS JUST THAT, ANYTHING ELSE...WE DO NOT APOLOGIZE FOR A DAMNED THING."

—SONNY BARGER, HELLS ANGEL

of their club, which featured actual members of the Venice charter of the Hells Angels as extras, go in search of the stolen bikes, kicking some ass with assorted motorcycle chains, fists, knives, and blunt instruments in the process. Dern's character, The Loser, ends up stealing a cop bike, gets in a chase with motorcycle cops, and gets shot. The club figures that The Loser would be better off partyin' with them rather than getting much-needed care in the hospital and they break him out of the joint. After some wild, party fun, Dern's character dies and the club, led by Fonda, has to find a place to bury him. The highlight of the film is its conclusion in a mountain retreat church where Fonda delivers a speech that has become a sort of a biker anthem: "We want to be free . . . free to ride our machines without being hassled by The Man. And we wanna get loaded!"

In the late 1960s, the media circus surrounding outlaw bikers was just beginning. The success of Hunter Thompson's book and the film *The Wild Angels* would only add fuel to the fire. It seemed that the world had a strange fascination with one percenters. The spectacle of a pack of choppers blasting down the highway amazed ordinary citizens even more than a circus coming to town.

After Roger Corman's *The Wild Angels* made millions, Hollywood pumped out a slew of down-and-dirty biker films. As always, filmmakers were eager to suck every penny out of a new movie genre and American International Pictures headed by Arkoff and Corman got to work producing low-dollar biker flicks. Of these films, *The Devil's Angels* (1967), starring John Cassavetes, stands out as a particularly revealing foray into the underbelly of bikerdom. Director Daniel Haller basically strings every outlaw biker cliché then known into a mish-mash of brawls, booze, and badass bikes. The Skulls, a fictitious MC club, spend a lot of time swilling brew, riding their scoots, and indulging their penchant for demolishing recreational vehicles. The Hells Angels Monterey rape trial was going on when this flick came out, and Haller exploited the publicity by having the leering Skulls accused of raping a whole town full of young ladies.

The flashier poster for *Hell's Angels '69*. The best thing about this movie is watching Sonny Barger, Terry the Tramp, and many of the real-life Hells Angels mentioned in Hunter Thompson's book, behaving themselves rather than acting and drinking a lot of beer in the background.

In classic western tradition, the bad guy bikers are driven out of town by the local lawmen but are then attacked by a bunch of rednecks, a theme that happens a lot in biker films. What comes across is some of the feeling of being in an outlaw club without any of the substance. The Skulls are seen as a tribe of wandering vagrants who ride their bikes in formation like some guerilla military group, sworn to fun and loyal to none.

Films such as *The Glory Stompers*, *Rebel Rousers*, *Born Losers,* and *The Cycle Savages* soon appeared at drive-ins across the country. Each produced plenty of misconceptions and outright falsehoods regarding myth of the outlaw biker.

Bikers began to turn up as the bad guys on television shows too, taking the place of Wild West outlaws. Being a biker was no longer a wholesome pursuit according to the mass media. By 1969 the biker exploitation film had pretty much fizzled out until producer/actor Peter Fonda relit the fuse with *Easy Rider*.

In the film, Captain America, played by Fonda, is a quiet reminder of what this

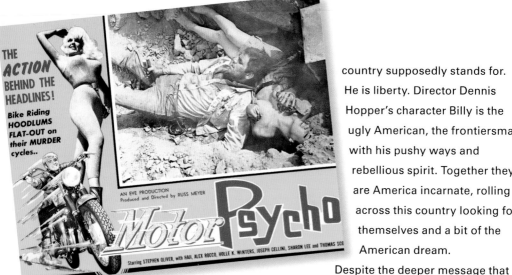

THE **ACTION** BEHIND THE HEADLINES!

Bike Riding HOODLUMS FLAT-OUT on their MURDER cycles..

AN EVE PRODUCTION
Produced and Directed by RUSS MEYER

Motor Psycho

Starring STEPHEN OLIVER, with HAJI, ALEX ROCCO, HOLLE K. WINTERS, JOSEPH CELLINI, SHARON LEE and THOMAS SCO

Russ Meyer's 1965 film *Motor Psycho* is similar to his better-known *Faster, Pussycat! Kill! Kill!* of the same year. The story involves a veterinarian whose wife is raped by bikers led by a sadistic Vietnam veteran. It's vet against vet in this sex and violence fun fest.

country supposedly stands for. He is liberty. Director Dennis Hopper's character Billy is the ugly American, the frontiersman with his pushy ways and rebellious spirit. Together they are America incarnate, rolling across this country looking for themselves and a bit of the American dream.

Despite the deeper message that America has sold out, American youth saw something else: free spirits on wild Harley choppers. Peter Fonda once told me he felt that the Woodstock generation lacked a movie that stood as their anthem. Fonda gave a whole generation an anthem with *Easy Rider*. There is something about those choppers floating down the highway that captures the essence of freedom.

By the mid-'70s many bikers had evolved into the black leather jacket– and greasy jeans–wearing, long-haired, tattooed, stinky, pot-smoking, chopper-riding stereotype that the media had painted for them. In fact, for a group made up of nonconformists, the bikers of that era all sort of looked and dressed alike. This uniformity extended to the motorcycle of choice for bikers everywhere: a Harley-Davidson. The preference for American motorcycles began in the early days, and when Indian went out of business in 1953, Harley-Davidson was the last American motorcycle company left.

ENTER THE ROLEX RIDERS

The Motor Company has always had an uneasy alliance with the outlaw community, first rejecting them outright, then seeing the value in capturing the rebel image, trying to make rebellion synonymous with Harley's motorcycles, as long as said "rebellion" was safe enough to pass muster with corporate lawyers.

For much of the twentieth century, the crudity and unreliability of Harley-Davidson motorcycles confined the company's customer base to riders who could overhaul their machines by the side of the road in the middle of the night using nothing but an adjustable Crescent wrench and a Zippo lighter—in other words one percenters. That changed in the early 1980s when Harley-Davidson introduced the Porsche-designed 1,340cc Evolution motor. The new aluminum V-twin motor was reliable and oil-tight compared to its cast-iron predecessors. For the first eighty years of its existence, Harleys were for people who weren't afraid to get dirty; overnight Harley-Davidson motorcycles became accessible to anyone with a large enough bank balance. The company began offering demo rides at their dealers, and in no time at all, upscale baby boomers with disposable income who had always had a soft spot in their hearts for Harleys bought the new machines in record numbers.

Suddenly, old-school bikers were sharing their outlaw steed with a legion of new riders made up of doctors and lawyers, accountants and software designers, all in brand spankin' new leathers and designer helmets. These upscale Rolex riders were tearing around on new Harleys that were dependable, didn't leak oil, and could cruise along for more than 100,000 miles without a motor rebuild.

It took a few years to pry loose the Shovelheads and Panheads from the fingers of the old guard, but by the mid-1990s old-school bikers and their Rich Urban Biker (Rubbie) counterparts were all riding Evo-powered machines to big motorcycle rallies such as Sturgis and Daytona and pretty much putting up with each other. Once old-school bikers saw that affluent new riders were loyal to the brand and that they were not going away any time soon, they cut them some slack for their shiny new Springer Softails and radio-blaring baggers.

A Vietnam veteran (not the same one as in *Motor Psycho*), played by Robert Fuller, brings his dead buddy's body home to his former girlfriend in *The Hard Ride*. Written and directed by Burt Topper, the film was also known as *Bury an Angel*. The vet runs into trouble with a rival biker gang when he is seen riding his dead buddy's chopper.

MOTORCYCLE MANIA

The biker nation was about to have the fifteen minutes of fame that Andy Warhol had promised us all. While biker flicks had been a staple at drive-in theaters back when there were still drive-in theaters, there had been relatively few television series focusing on bikers over the years. For a short time in 1969 NBC's *Then Came Bronson* filled the bill and many thousands of new bikers were born after watching laconic drifter Jim Bronson (Michael Parks) ride his Harley Sportster through picturesque America. In the 1990s, a syndicated series called *Renegade* followed Reno Raines (Lorenzo Lamas) as a renegade cop turned bounty hunter astride a Harley Softail. Though the two TV series were worlds apart in concept, they both focused on the freedom found on the open road on two wheels.

In 2000, TV producer Hugh King pitched a television documentary idea to The Discovery Channel called *Motorcycle Mania*, which followed the exploits of bad boy bike builder Jesse James. *Motorcycle Mania* generated the highest ratings ever for a cable network show. Naturally, *Motorcycle Mania II* and *Motorcycle Mania III* followed, as did the *Monster Garage* TV series, and metal maverick Jesse James became a household name.

At the turn of the millennium, motorcycle sales were on an upward climb, factory custom choppers were selling like hot cakes, and The Discovery Channel had a hit on its hands. Cashing in on the trend, Pilgrim Films & Television Inc. out of New York shot a pilot with a relatively new custom bike shop in Rock Tavern, New York, called Orange County Choppers (OCC). The owner of the shop, Paul Teutul Senior, was a lifelong biker and ironworker. His son, Paul Junior, was skilled in metalworking and in fabricating custom bikes.

American Chopper featured the crew at Orange County Choppers smashing and bashing their way into America's heart. The Teutuls'

"THE MOST IMPORTANT THING IS TO HAVE A GOOD RELATIONSHIP WITH THE BIKE... YOU HAVE TO UNDERSTAND WHAT SHE WANTS. I THINK OF A MOTORCYCLE AS A WOMAN."

—VALENTINO ROSSI, MOTOGP WORLD CHAMPION

hour-long shows revolved around building highly customized theme bikes against the clock. These bikes resembled everything from fire engines to space shuttles.

Viewers loved the idea of blue-collar workers making good and enjoyed watching the Teutuls rise to stardom. As their bike business picked up, life was apparently good for the Teutuls. The message of *American Chopper* was less about bike building and more about making it big in America.

The Discovery Channel execs realized that viewers had a true love affair with custom motorcycles and developed yet another TV series with Hugh King and Thom Beers of Original Productions known as *The Great Biker Build-Off*, featuring such diverse master bike builders as Billy Lane, Paul Yaffe, Dave Perewitz, Indian Larry, Mitch Bergeron, Chica, Jerry Covington, Mondo Porras of Denver's Choppers, Kendall Johnson, the Detroit Brothers, and many others.

Thus the stage was set for the television series *Sons of Anarchy.* Like the Hells Angels, the fictional Sons of Anarchy have charters all over the world, but the series focuses on the founding charter known as Sons of Anarchy Motorcycle Club, Redwood Original, or SAMCRO. Series creator Kurt Sutter says the storyline of *Sons of Anarchy* is actually based on Shakespeare's *Hamlet*, the ageless tale of the sins of the father being visited upon the son.

And all of this led to the pasteurization of the outlaw biker. In one generation we have seen the rabid wolves of bikerdom get stripped of their fangs in favor of a brighter, whiter, on-camera smile. The phenomenon of seeing one percenters signing autographs

The biker's bible for more than forty-five years, *Easyriders* issue No. 1 hit the newsstands in June 1971 and changed the face of motorcycle magazines forever.

(Sonny Barger signs books at Barnes & Noble stores) is a bit like people lining up to meet Geronimo or taking a photo with the freshly killed lion. People now attend bike shows wearing *Sons of Anarchy* T-shirts, sweatshirts, or even leather vests adorned with the SAMCRO colors and back patches. To understand how real one percenters react to this, imagine if civilians showed up to a law enforcement convention dressed as cops. It wouldn't go over well.

"HARLEYS DON'T LEAK OIL; THEY MARK THEIR TERRITORY."

–UNKNOWN

Fortunately an entirely new generation of biker has emerged on the scene in the last ten years and they are about something. This new rider truly lives, eats, and breathes motorcycles. These people love the biker lifestyle and all it represents. They were raised reading *Easyriders* magazine and have their heads on straight. The seeds of rebellion that were planted decades ago are now flourishing among this new breed of riders.

Photographer Ben Zales and his crew of motorized miscreants camp out in Death Valley.

> **"THE ROAD NEVER ENDS ... ONLY OUR VISION DOES."**
>
> —AMIT REDDY, AUTHOR

2
THE MODERN SAVAGE

♠

M By 2009 veteran bikers began noticing a n
breed of biker on the scene, guys in their
twenties and thirties who seemed as if the
had somehow teleported through time from the 1970s in
Haight-Ashbury. These guys rode oil-dripping Panhead and
Shovelhead Harley choppers with rigid frames and ultra-hi
sissybars and ape hanger handlebars, with Mexican blanke
tied to the bars carrying makeshift camping gear. Some of
their rusty scooters were painted in odd pastel colors with
stickers of unicorns and rainbows on them. Some of the gu
wore beards and sombreros, or maybe a luchador wrestlin
mask and white Ray-Ban sunglasses with checkered bow ti
Still others looked like a David Mann painting had come to
beer-farting life!

If you were a family in a minivan, however, taking a
Sunday drive through the Black Hills during the Sturgis rall

It's not what you ride, it's that you ride, as this lineup of chopper iron proves.
From old-school Shovelheads to Hondas, it's all good.

and these guys came blasting by you in formation on their wicked-looking choppers, you might think the Hells Angels had just roared past you. But a closer look clearly reveals that this new breed is just out to have a good time. In that way, they are closer to the original idea of the Boozefighters than any one percenter club.

OPPOSITE: Scotty, one of the members of the Douche Larouche Motorcycle Club, shows us how to party in his luchador wrestling mask. ABOVE: Whatever is happening here, you can rest assured that Mom would be proud.

Today's biker probably grew up reading magazines such as *Street Chopper*, *The Horse*, *Biker*, *Easyriders*, and *DICE*, watching biker flicks, and they truly live to ride. Their entire lives are tied up and wrapped around motorcycles. They honor everything from the glory days of bikerdom and think that the real life hardcore bikers from back in the day are living gods. But unlike

ABOVE: Douche Larouche Grand Wizard Jason Wilson's Shovelhead adorned with briny denizens of the deep for the Easyriders Bike Show. OPPOSITE: The Golden Gnome, a.k.a. Goldie, is a regular on every Douche Larouche MC run. Not just a good-luck charm, he points the way to depravity.

the bikers from back in the day, most of the new breed went to college, have good jobs, and many have families. The more you get to know them, the more you realize that many have high-tech careers, truly quirky senses of humor, and many are like warped versions of hipsters.

WHAT'S A HIPSTER?

Hipsters are almost as difficult to define as this new breed of biker. Bikers and hipsters do have a few things in common. Let's look at the stereotype of the hipster: skinny jeans, flannel shirt, fedora or wool cap, luxurious beard, tattoos, possibly vegan, definitely eat organic, probably gluten-free, definitely drinks PBR tall boys. They dig old tech like typewriters, film cameras, electric fans, and vinyl.

Now I'm not saying that our new bikers are necessarily related to hipster culture, but there do seem to be some similarities. In his 2011 book *HipsterMattic*, author Matt Granfield described hipster culture:

> *While mainstream society of the 2000s [decade] had been busying itself with reality television, dance music, and locating the whereabouts of Britney Spears's underpants, an uprising was quietly and conscientiously taking place behind the scenes. Long-forgotten styles of clothing, beer, cigarettes, and music were becoming popular again. Retro was cool, the environment was precious, and old was the new new. Kids wanted to wear Sylvia Plath's cardigans and Buddy Holly's glasses—they reveled in the irony of making something so nerdy so cool. They wanted to live sustainably and eat organic gluten-free grains. Above all, they wanted to be recognized for being different—to diverge from the mainstream and carve a cultural niche all for themselves. For this new generation, style wasn't something you could buy in a department store; it became something you found in a thrift shop, or, ideally, made yourself. The way to be cool wasn't to look like a television star; it was to look like as though you'd never seen television.*

THE DOUCHE LAROUCHE

In 2010 I met a group of cycle-loving miscreants known as the Douche LaRouche Motorcycle Club out of southern California (naturally). If you watch the film *The Wild One* and check out the antics of both Marlon Brando's comical biker club The Black Rebels as well as Lee Marvin's ratty bike club The Beetles, you'll get a taste of what it's like to spend an afternoon with the Douche LaRouche. These boys are out to have a good time and have an infinite imagination when it comes to finding ways to live large and entertain themselves. These guys exemplify the

This gorgeous Flathead was one of many righteous choppers seen in the DLMC's "Enchantment Under the Sea" exhibit at the Easyriders Anaheim Bike Show.

"WE HAD ONE RULE THAT SAID YOU HAVE TO BE 'BOOZEFIGHTERS UP' AT ALL TIMES. IF YOU PASSED OUT, YOU'D BETTER LAND ON YOUR FACE, 'CAUSE IF YOU LANDED ON YOUR BACK AND COVERED THAT BOOZEFIGHTERS PATCH, YOU WERE OUT OF THE CLUB."

–NORMAN, BOOZEFIGHTER

new breed of biker I'm talking about in this book. They aren't here for a long time, they're here for a good time.

The Douche LaRouche showed up at our Easyriders Anaheim Bike Show in 2011 aboard rag-tag choppers, with an idea that would put them on the *Easyriders* map. Cary Brobeck and bike builder Jason Wilson of Sacred Steel decided to create a camping scene for their custom motorcycle display. They took a big section of bike show spaces, dumped wheelbarrows of dirt on the cement floor, erected a tent, made a fake fire pit, drank a whole lot of beer so that they could litter the camp scene with empty beer cans, tossed old 1970s and '80s back issues of *Easyriders* magazine on the site, and arranged the bikes so that it looked like a couple of the old choppers had crashed into each other and fallen over. There might have been a mannequin involved. The guys at the Hells Angels booth right across from the big camping scene weren't so happy about it though and complained to our bike show head honcho, John Green. John made the boys promise to clean up every last speck of dirt after the show, which they did.

The hardest part was how to create an even wackier, sicker display for the following year. The Douche LaRouche came up with a brilliant Enchantment Under the Sea theme for the 2012 show. Called "Deepsea Bromance," it

ABOVE: This prom theme gone bad was actually called "Deepsea Bromance" and featured a large backdrop that was painted to look like the ocean floor. OPPOSITE: The Douche Larouche boys brought in truckloads of sand and a bubble machine to take their undersea scene to the next level of frothy goodness.

DLMC Original Cary Brobeck, who is also the editor of *WRENCH* magazine and a regular on the Discovery Channel's *Sacred Steel* TV series, blasts down the road to adventure in Mexico on his faithful Panhead.

"WE STICK UP FOR OUR OWN, RIGHT OR WRONG.
THINK ABOUT IT. IF YOUR OWN BROTHER IS
GETTING HIS ASS KICKED, DO YOU GIVE A DAMN
IF HE IS IN THE WRONG OR NOT? FUCK IT IF
HE IS WRONG, FUCK IT IF HE IS RIGHT; YOU'RE
GOING TO JUMP IN FOR HIM."

—SONNY BARGER, HELLS ANGEL

featured a large backdrop that was painted to look like the ocean floor, a twisted episode of *Sponge Bob Square Pants* with quasi-homoerotic undertones. The boys dumped a ton of sand in front of a backdrop painted with mermaids and mermen, colorful fish, lobsters, starfish, sea horses, and even a sunken treasure. Then they festooned their choppers with seaweed and plastic fish. They fired up a bubble machine, which pissed off the Vagos MC. Apparently bubbles float around indiscriminately, causing soapy discharge to collect on expensive custom paint jobs. The Douche LaRouche naturally won best display and a special trophy for the best old-school oil-leaking chopper. The presentation of this award involved dragging a new member of the club behind a chopper as part of his initiation.

"TV HAS MADE STARS OUT OF A LOT OF BIKE BUILDERS, BUT IT TAKES A LOT MORE THAN A PERFORMANCE ON TV TO BE A CUSTOM BIKE BUILDER."

—DAVE PEREWITZ, MASTER BUILDER

RITES OF PASSAGE

Initiation rituals are an element shared by both the traditional outlaw clubs and the new breed of outlaws. The indoctrination into full membership of an outlaw biker club embodies elements of the rites of passage that are as old as humankind, and these rituals are, if not copied outright, at least alluded to in spirit by the new breed of clubs. That's because the same impulses are driving the new breed bikers as drove their predecessors. The new breed finds brotherhood and camaraderie within his motorcycle club just as bikers always have.

The motorcycle club is just one of the ways that modern men re-create the rites of passage. Another is tattooing and modifying their bodies. Tattoos offer a permanent way to add symbols of rites of passage onto our very skin. Whether through tattoos, body piercing, or joining motorcycle clubs, human beings who don't fit into societal norms will always find ways to stretch the boundaries and live outside the status

OPPOSITE: "Listen Ryan," Chatty spat, "you have got to stop drinking gasoline, bro." BELOW: Dayten likes to enhance his ensemble with a stylish Mexican blanket and an *Easyriders* shirt.

"I USED TO WORK AT A HARLEY SHOP CALLED DR. CARL'S HOG HOSPITAL IN VENICE BEACH. THAT WAS MY FIRST REAL JOB. NOW I TRAVEL AROUND WITH FRIENDS AND DISCOVER NEW THINGS ON MOTORCYCLES FOR THE AMC TV SERIES RIDE."

—NORMAN REEDUS, ACTOR AND BIKER

quo. Often they are following well-established family traditions. Some of the young guns were raised by bikers and are following the lifestyle they picked up from their fathers. Nothing bonds a father and son together like the shared love of motorcycles.

THE BIG THREE

Rebellion takes many forms. Certainly we have all heard of the big three one percenter clubs that head the most-wanted list: the Hells Angels, Outlaws, and Bandidos.

According to Hells Angel Sonny Barger, he and a group of friends were riding around Oakland, California, wearing the death's head patch and calling themselves Hells Angels back in 1957. But they found out that there were two other clubs in California using the same logo and calling themselves the same thing. One of the clubs was from San Bernadino, the remnants of the Pissed Off Bastards, who, after the Hollister incident, changed their name to the Hells Angels in 1948. This charter is generally thought to have been the first chapter of the red and white.

The Hells Angels incorporated in 1966: "Dedicated to the promotion and advancement of motorcycle riding, motorcycle clubs, motorcycle highway safety, and all phases of motorcycling and motorcycle driving." The club trademarked their logo in 1972 and their name in the 1980s. Worldwide, the Hells Angels are said to have more than sixty charters in North America and nearly forty in other countries.

The Bandidos began in 1966 out of Houston, Texas, as a group of blue-collar motorcycle lovers and have since expanded to become a global one percenter club. Their first chapter in Australia was the Sydney Chapter, started in 1984. Today they have more than 250

OPPOSITE TOP: Doug rockin' along on his rusty, we mean "trusty," Panhead and wearing classic biker boat shoes. OPPOSITE: Ryan Cox hangs with his buds at Newcomb Ranch, a biker diner in the Angeles National Forest.

"WHEN I'M WORKING ON A BIKE AND EVERYTHING COMES TOGETHER PERFECTLY, WHEN I SEE THE VISION I HAVE IN MY HEAD APPEARING IN METAL REALITY, I THINK TO MYSELF THAT I AM ON MY RAILS. AT THOSE TIMES MY LIFE IS FOLLOWING THE TRACK IT'S SUPPOSED TO FOLLOW, THAT I'M DOING WHAT I'M MEANT TO BE DOING."

—BILLY LANE, BIKE BUILDER

members in Australia alone. The Bandidos MC claim to have more than ninety chapters in the United States, ninety chapters in Europe, and fifteen chapters in Australia and Southeast Asia.

American chapters exist in Texas, Louisiana, Mississippi, Alabama, Arkansas, New Mexico, Colorado, Nebraska, Nevada, Montana, Oklahoma, Wyoming, South Dakota, Utah, Idaho, Washington State, and others. The club has also expanded into Germany, Denmark, Norway, Sweden, Finland, Belgium, Italy, Luxembourg, France, and the Channel Isles of Great Britain.

In 1935, the McCook Outlaws Motorcycle Club was established out of Matilda's Bar in McCook, Illinois. The club grew to include members from all over the Chicago area, changing its name and logo in 1950. The first Florida chapter was sanctioned in 1967, and in 1977 the first chapter outside the United States was established when the Satan's Choice of Canada became an

OPPOSITE: Sometimes you have to push your bike. Here we see Gus pushing his Flathead chopper *El Mysterioso* somewhere around Yosemite, California. The mystery is whether it's going to start. BELOW: Rad Ryan having a little rowdy fun with his Knucklehead chopper. Did you know rigid long bikes can do wheelies?

Outlaws chapter. The first European chapter of the Outlaws MC was born in France in 1993, the Australian Outlaws were formed in 1994, and the independent Belgium chapter joined the American Outlaws Association (AOA) in 1999.

Since 2000, English, Welsh, and Norwegian Outlaw chapters were added, followed by new chapters in Ireland, Germany, Thailand, and a second chapter in Sweden. The Outlaws MC continued to expand throughout the USA, Canada, Great Britain, Poland, Norway, Italy, and even Russia.

It is clear to see that the very American rebel notion of the one percenter motorcycle club has expanded throughout the world despite the machinations of the popular media, police harassment, or changing moral values. In today's pasteurized, germ-free consciousness and industrialized, mindless laborers,

OPPOSITE: Sherm looks like he roared right out of *Easy Rider*. You can almost hear Steppenwolf's "Born to be Wild" in your head. ABOVE: On the other hand, Sherm and his lady passenger look more like a living example of David Mann's famous painting *The Ghost Rider*.

"FASTER, FASTER, FASTER, UNTIL THE THRILL OF SPEED OVERCOMES THE FEAR OF DEATH."

—HUNTER THOMPSON

the world needs the one percenter more than ever. In a time when so many of us go to work every day hating our jobs and feeling disconnected from our lives, we all need to throw a leg over a throbbing motorcycle and raise a little hell every now and then.

RIDERS OF EVERY FLAVOR

Besides one percenter clubs, there are motorcycle clubs of every possible flavor imaginable. For instance there's the Antique Motorcycle Club of America, Bikers for Christ, the BMW Motorcycle Owners of America, Canadian Army Veteran Motorcycle Unit, Cycle Queens of America, Combat Veterans Motorcycle Association, Freewheelers EVS out of England, the Harley Owners Group, Holy Riders, and of course the Jewish Motorcycle Alliance. Founded in 2004, the Jewish Motorcycle Alliance has more than 2,500 Jewish motorcyclists in it around the world. Riders of any denomination on any brand of bike are welcome.

You'll find the Madras Bulls in India, the ladies of the Motor Maids, and the Night Wolves of Russia. We ran an article on the Night Wolves club in *Easyriders* a while back. They started out as rock 'n' roll music and Harley fans back in 1983, holding illegal rock concerts in Moscow. They were the first bike club in the USSR and have established chapters in the Ukraine, Latvia, Germany, Bulgaria, Romania, Serbia, and Macedonia.

Other interesting non-one percenter clubs are the Moped Army and the Patriot Guard Riders, who are known for attending the funerals of members of the US military, firefighters, and police. Then there are the Rainbow MC from San Francisco, the Shrewsbury Motocross Club from England, Triumph Owners Club, Ulysses Club from Australia, the Vintage Motorcycle Club, Women in the Wind MC, and Leather & Lace MC.

OPPOSITE: Troy, Matt, and Justin lead a crew on old American iron on a 666-mile ride. BELOW: Jason blasts down a perfect stretch of road on his Knucklehead chopper.

"A MOTORCYCLE IS AN INDEPENDENT THING."

—RYAN HURST, ACTOR, *SONS OF ANARCHY*

3
EASY-
RIDERS

♠

People under the age of twenty-five might not believe this, but there was a time before cell phones and the internet. There was a time when all the knowledge ever collected by humankind was not instantly available at one's fingertips, a time people had to do research. There were big buildings called *libraries* that housed thousands of paper books found through using the torture device known as the Dewey Decimal Classification system.

During those dark ages there was no way to, say, find out about custom motorcycles because chopper magazines and biker lifestyle magazines did not exist. Before 1970, the only information gleaned from magazines or newspapers were articles that blamed bikers for the downfall of civilization.

The only time you ever heard about motorcycle clubs was in print articles that painted bikers as monsters, ravenous, flesh-eating fiends out to burn down your towns, to rape your daughters, and take down our sacred American way of life. As the old newspaper saying goes, "If it bleeds, it leads."

The guys gather at Panamint Springs in Death Valley for a group photo to commemorate the Death Valley Run.

ABOVE: Ben on his "Beauty" CB750 chopper riding the canyons near Malibu, California. OPPOSITE: Al's gorgeous original Knucklehead in Redlands, California. This is what a classic Harley looks like before it gets chopped.

Motorcycle magazines back in the mid-1960s were boring little product placement venues, mostly for Honda and Yamaha. There was no motorcycle magazine that was about the actual people who build these crazy machines. But that was about to change.

In the years following World War II, riders stripped stock Harleys to lighten them for speed. These were called *bobbers*; what we refer to as *choppers* started showing up in the 1960s, but these long, spindly motorcycles were rare. That began to change during the psychedelic hippy era, especially after the film *Easy Rider*.

Up until the Vietnam War, Americans had been taught to do their civic duty and go to war for their country. It was the honorable, patriotic thing to do. Line up and die. The late '50s and early '60s ushered in the first generation to go to college in mass in order to have a better life than their parents. When you go to college, you learn things, your horizons expand, and you might just start thinking for yourself.

"WE ARE A GROUP OF COMPLETE INDIVIDUALS, AND I
MEAN INDIVIDUALS. EVERY ONE OF US HAS A DIFFERENT
REASON FOR BEING WHO WE ARE. THE ONLY THING WE
AGREE ON IS OUR LOVE FOR THE CLUB. THAT, AND OUR
LOVE FOR MOTORCYCLES."

—SONNY BARGER, HELLS ANGEL

Anthony and Ben's Beauty and the Beast Honda 750 four-cylinder choppers. These were super popular in the 1970s.

ABOVE: The crew's campsite in Panamint Springs on the Death Valley Run. Looks like this shot could have been taken in the 1970s. OPPOSITE: Cary Brobeck, the magnificent editor of *WRENCH* magazine, on his Panhead chopper on the Kern River Run.

Our leaders don't want us to think for ourselves because then we're less likely to join the army and get shipped overseas to kill people for oil. Our leaders want us to line up and salute! They don't want us to question authority. Vietnam was the first American war in which kids who were draft age stood up and said, "Uh, excuse me, sir, I don't think this is a very good idea. I mean, why are we going over there, again? I don't want to hurt anyone." Since going to college postponed being drafted, even more people decided to go to college.

This set the stage for the emergence of the sex-drugs-and-rock-'n'-roll generation. People were doing psychedelic drugs and having orgies. We lived through Vietnam, Kent State, Watergate, hippies, yippies, and Woodstock. Into this powder keg, Peter Fonda dropped a lit match in the form of the film *Easy*

"OUR MOTTO IS 'ALL ON ONE AND ONE ON ALL.' WHEN YOU MESS WITH AN ANGEL, YOU'LL HAVE TWENTY-FIVE OF US ON YOUR NECK."

—A FRISCO ANGEL

Rider. College-age kids came out of the theaters wanting to be free, free to ride their machines without being hassled by the man. And they wanted to get loaded!

Easy Rider came to stand for personal freedom. While this may not have been Peter Fonda's or Dennis Hopper's intent with the film, it is what stuck in the craw of America's youth. Suddenly a bunch of people in their twenties wanted to taste the freedom found while riding a custom chopper.

BIKER 101

The majority of these would-be riders knew nothing about motorcycles; their fathers were not bikers and even fewer had fathers who were outlaw bikers. How did these guys find out how to be a biker? There was no biker school to teach them what kind of leather jacket or engineer boots to buy, or that black jeans are best because they don't show the inevitable grease and oil stains that accompany oil-leaking bikes that constantly break down.

Then and now, the only way for new riders to become indoctrinated into the world of bikers is to hang out with bikers. You'll find them at bike shops, bars, and motorcycle runs and rallies. Clearly there was need for biker lifestyle and chopper magazines, magazines that not only taught readers how to build choppers, but how to live the life. *Easyriders* contributor John "Rogue" Herlihy wrote about the magazine *Colors*, which predated *Easyriders*:

Colors **is a very hard to find, short-lived magazine, and predated Easyriders** *summer 1971 debut. It was founded and edited by Phil Castle, a biker who ran a fuel oil delivery company in* **New Jersey** *while trying to make the magazine a success.*

Colors *was primarily focused on the East Coast bike clubs and events, as that was its home turf, so to speak. But, the money ran out before the mag caught on, and by the end of 1971 it had folded, after only five or so issues. It also suffered from poor distribution, as some newsstands, hypocritically, wouldn't carry it, and the first issue was banned in a few states.*

Colors *was a good magazine, especially considering that the people involved were bikers, not journalists making their living from publishing. The idea was to have a voice, and tell it like it is. Let people know what was going on, and in many cases, the other side of the story. The stories and information released to the news media by law enforcement and the government was often times misleading or untrue.*

OPPOSITE: Jason Webber put together this killer example of a Cone Shovelhead for a customer in Anaheim, California. BELOW: A profile shot of Dayten's Ironhead chopper. He built this bike in his garage in Thousand Oaks, California.

"I WAS FAMOUS FROM BIRTH."

—PETER FONDA

It was also going to be a tool to support our efforts in repealing the mandatory helmet laws and other injustices to motorcyclists. And in a way, it did do what it was intended to, by being imitated by larger publishers. The format carried over, and we were in an even better position to inform the bikers of America what was going on.

As the title Colors *and the side bar "Motorcycle Club's Bible" (later changed to "The Non-Conforming Motorcyclist's Bible") make clear, it was oriented to, and focused on, the outlaw clubs. It was filled with an abundance of black and white photos of various club colors, bikes, members, mamas, hangouts, and it even had some tech-oriented articles. Its statement of purpose, and format, given in the first issue (May 1970), reads as follows:*

This is your magazine. That's right, at last someone has come out with a magazine that is not afraid to be called an outlaw magazine. We will not hide behind technical articles or motorcycle manufacturer's sales talk on those foreign bikes. COLORS *magazine will not have an 80% AMA background.*

We do not care which citizens won what AMA sanctioned race or event. Instead we will feature stories, articles, pictures, and so forth of so-called outlaws and clubs.

We will not exclude all foreign bikes from our pages so long as they are directly or indirectly connected to a club, as there are some pretty hot foreign bikes that have been made into some beautiful custom jobs. Nor do we want to feature only choppers as there are many outlaws who do not ride choppers.

We will print any news of your club that you would approve of, as well as pictures, articles and events having to do with clubs.

COLORS *will also feature interviews, technical material and some cheesecake for you red blooded studs.* COLORS *will be glad to print any gripe you may have or any pictures of your bikes, club or its members if you will send some to us.*

This is a general idea of the format of COLORS *(your) magazine, and its success depends on your help and patronage.*

OPPOSITE: Dayten and his sweet Ironhead are ready to ride the mean streets in downtown L.A.

EASYRIDERS

Easyriders magazine debuted in June 1971. *Easyriders* was not specifically aimed at one percenters but at the wider biker culture audience of the time. After the success of the film *Easy Rider* (it made an estimated 60 million domestic in 1969), even Harley-Davidson took notice of the chopper trend and came out with what they called a factory custom. Designer Willie G. Davidson married a Sportster front end to an FL frame, gave it a Sparkling America red-white-and-blue paint scheme, and created the Super Glide. At the same time the Super Glide hit the streets, two bikers from Minnesota moved to Southern California and made two-wheeled history.

Gearheads Mil Blair and Joe Teresi teamed up with magazine editor Lou Kimzey to produce a lifestyle-driven magazine that would appeal to bikers. Lou had been riding choppers since they were called bobbers and motorcycle clubs had names like the 13 Rebels, Galloping Gooses, and Deuces Wild. Lou had been an editor of drag racing and men's magazines, creating such titles as *Drag Racing*, *Drag Strip*, and *Big Bike*. The two-wheeled trio wanted their new magazine to be completely different than any motorcycle magazine on the planet

TOP: Doug and his "Million Dollar Baby" Cone motor Shovel against a brick wall in downtown Los Angeles. OPPOSITE: "It's a chopper, baby!" Doug's scooter in the middle of the road overlooking the L.A. skyline.

ABOVE: Eddie on his sick Cone Shovelhead wheelie machine. RIGHT: Adam and a hitch-hiking babe seen in the canyons of Malibu on a foggy morning. OPPOSITE: A candid photo of an unknown biker on his Evo-powered Sportster chopper along the Kern River.

at the time and succeeded with the irreverent and madcap format that would become known as *Easyriders* magazine.

Joe Teresi was the technical editor of *Big Bike* and, along with bike builder and parts fabricator Mil Blair, designed many aftermarket parts for people who wanted to build choppers of their own. Mil was also into cameras and acted as the first photo editor of *Easyriders*. Along with these three paisanos (hence the company's name Paisano Publications), Don Pfeil signed on as editor-at-large and produced editorials capturing the passion of the chopper experience.

Teresi believed that motorcycle magazines of that time showcased bikes but not the people who built or rode them. *Easyriders* was aimed at being a

"THE BEST THING ABOUT THE HELLS ANGELS IS THAT WE DON'T LIE TO EACH OTHER … HELL, MOST PEOPLE YOU MEET WON'T TELL YOU THE TRUTH ABOUT ANYTHING."

—ZORRO, THE ONLY BRAZILIAN HELLS ANGEL IN THE 1960s

Jason Wilson of the Discovery Channel's *Sacred Steel* on his Generator Shovelhead chopper in front of his East L.A. shop.

magazine that captured the people behind the custom bikes as well as the wild lifestyle that surrounded them. It would turn out to be a winning combination of custom motorcycles and real bikers, seen by both bikers and the general public for the first time in a magazine devoted to the biker lifestyle.

Just as Fonda and Hopper's film *Easy Rider* acted as a microcosm of the hippie and biker culture, so *Easyriders* focused the rebellious biker lifestyle and defined it. The first issue didn't offer a biker chick on the cover, just a wild chop job. Soon, the team figured out that sex sells and made sure there was always a pretty girl seen with a custom motorcycle on the cover.

Easyriders had a definite and tweaked point of view right from the start, from the "Takin' It Easy" column of bizarre news stories and weird tidbits, to mind-bending art direction and quirky cartoons. They even invented oddball characters like Miraculous Mutha who answered sex questions and letters to the lovelorn. The first issue jumped off the shelves.

OPPOSITE LEFT TOP: Sherm's Generator Shovelhead motor. OPPOSITE LEFT MIDDLE: Ben's Honda CB750 four-cylinder chopper motor. OPPOSITE LEFT BOTTOM: Dayten's trusty, rusty Ironhead Sportster motor. OPPOSITE RIGHT TOP: Jason's "triclops" Harley Knucklehead motor. The first real Big Twin. OPPOSITE RIGHT BOTTOM: Jason's Panhead motor. To me, this is the most beautiful motor Harley ever made. BELOW: Jason Wilson and the Douche Larouche Motorcycle Club cruise through the tunnels of downtown Los Angeles.

"IF YOU WANT TO BE HAPPY FOR A DAY, DRINK. IF YOU WANT TO BE HAPPY FOR A YEAR, MARRY. IF YOU WANT TO BE HAPPY FOR LIFE, RIDE A MOTORCYCLE."

—UNKNOWN

But the magazine wasn't just about wild times; very early on *Easyriders* established ABATE, which at the time stood for A Brotherhood Against Totalitarian Enactments. Today the organization stands for A Brotherhood Aimed Toward Education and promotes rider education over governmental legislation. The idea was to create a body that policed governmental policies regarding custom motorcycles and acted as a watchdog for new laws that restrict biker's rights and freedom. At present, ABATE has chapters all over the country with membership in the tens of thousands.

The magazine was, and is, a sounding board for readers who kept the biker lifestyle alive through Harley's lean AMF years. *Easyriders* readers have always been very vocal. There's never been any guesswork in finding out what they want, and so *Easyriders* success has been the success of the American biker, independent, loyal, and proud.

Easyriders has always been about reflecting the custom motorcycling world, and as the custom bike scene changed and evolved, so did *Easyriders* magazine. By 1980 the rag was already going through refinements, adding more tech tips and legislative news, offering more color photography, more big bike events, runs, and parties, more gorgeous gals, and wilder art. Cool products produced by bikers for bikers began to appear beginning with *Easyriders* T-shirts, belt buckles, boots, and more. This would soon mutate into an entire products division, including everything a biker might need, from leathers and riding gear, to tools and bike lifts.

Bikers have changed dramatically in the forty-five years since *Easyriders* first appeared. The public perception of bikers has run the gamut, from post–World War II vets with bomber jackets, raising a little hell, to crazed long-haired maniacs on loud choppers. Today, many of those same rowdy hell-raisers who were scary, Panhead ridin' bikers of the 1970s and '80s are now the dudes you

OPPOSITE: Jeff and his long Knucklehead chopper are livin' the dream, overlooking the Pacific Ocean in Malibu, California. ABOVE: Jeff on his Panhead chopper equipped with a classy Sugar Bear springer front end on the Kern River Run.

ABOVE: Luke doing some roadside wrenchin' on his Panhead on the Pacific Coast Highway. Hey, breakdowns are part of the fun, right? OPPOSITE TOP: Mark takes a break at a gas station while on Nash's Hell Ride. This is what you look like if your bike won't kick over. OPPOSITE: Mark roars off on his custom Panhead during Nash's Hell Ride.

see puttin' to Sturgis on a big, comfy bagger. They usually limp from all the years they kick-started their bikes and their knees have been trashed.

The magazine has been about backyard builders who create custom bikes by hand, the old-fashioned way, but also includes big name builders that have become super stars thanks to the miracle of television. Though it all, *Easyriders* has been a lens through which the riding world has seen itself. We reflect what's going on out there in the world. Sometimes that's good, sometimes not. *Easyriders* has succeeded because it is not about nuts and bolts, parts, and pieces. Rather, the magazine is about the very real people who have an abiding passion for motorcycles. Bikers have oil running in their veins and live for the thrill of riding their bikes. *Easyriders* is dedicated to those guys and gals who truly live to ride and ride to live.

One thing old and new bikers seem to have in common is their love and respect for bikers of old and *Easyriders* magazine. They wax poetic on how their

"I WENT THROUGH ALL THAT SCHOOL AND FAMILY JAZZ. IT'S ALL CRAP. BOY, I'M GLAD THE ANGELS TOOK ME IN! I DON'T EVER WANT TO BE ANYTHING BUT AN ANGEL AND THAT'S IT."

—A HELLS ANGEL

ABOVE: Ryan Cox's super clean rigid Panhead. This look never goes out of style. OPPOSITE: Ryan Grossman and his easy ridin' Knucklehead long bike in Martinez, California.

dads let them look at their old back issues when they were growing up. The biker rag was always in the garage or in the shitter. In a straight-laced world, *Easyriders* told them it was okay to be a nonconformist. It was good to be a rebel.

Also at the top of their list is an abiding love for biker lifestyle artist David Mann, whose art was seen in every issue of *Easyriders* since issue three. I often hear pseudo-bikers spout off about "Keepin' it real!" without having any idea what that means. Let me tell you, David Mann was the real deal. He kept it real.

DAVID MANN

David Mann created his very first painting of the motorcycle culture back in 1963. That painting, *Hollywood Run*, accompanied him and his customized 1948 Panhead to the Kansas City Custom Car Show. There, he met Tiny, an outlaw motorcycle club member, and a close friendship that would last a lifetime was born.

Tiny sent a photograph of David's painting to Ed "Big Daddy" Roth, a famous car and bike customizer and the publisher of the short-lived *Chopper* magazine. Ed bought the painting for eighty-five dollars and David's career as "the Norman

Rockwell of the biker world" began. He went on to do ten more paintings for Roth, who published them in his magazines and offered them as posters.

In 1971, David saw his first issue of *Easyriders* magazine and an ad for artists, cartoonists, and illustrators caught his eye. The publisher and editor both liked his work and he was hired. His centerspread art capturing the biker lifestyle illuminated the magazine for more than thirty years until his death on September 11, 2004.

David Mann's art is still loved by bikers everywhere because of his uncanny knack for finding the essence of the lifestyle he loved. His work derived from personal experiences and David's honesty showed in every painting. Many of the wild custom designs seen on the motorcycles in David's paintings actually inspired fabricators to create more extreme choppers. He would exaggerate the rake and stretch of a frame, extend a Springer front end much longer than was popular, or make ape hangers and sissybars reach the sky. Soon, builders would replicate David's designs, making custom bikes that were wilder and wilder.

David Mann's art continues to inspire the new breed of biker. One bike builder in particular, Jason Wilson, had a vision: create a real life, fire-breathing replica of a bike found in one of David Mann's paintings. Wilson owns Sacred Steel Customs in Southern California and is one of the founders of the Douche LaRouche. He has a lifelong love for motorcycles, kustom kulture, old-school chopper builders, and David Mann.

"THE BEST ALARM CLOCK IS SUNSHINE ON CHROME."

—UNKNOWN

Sacred Steel Customs is a haven for like-minded bikers seeking brotherhood and a righteous shop that builds honest-to-god killer kustom choppers. The shop's popularity has grown to the point that in September 2016, Discovery Channel aired *Sacred Steel*. In the first of six episodes, Jason built a chopper inspired by *Zodiac*, a David Mann painting that Ed "Big Daddy" Roth featured in *Choppers* magazine. Sacred Steel's Zodiac chopper, which features an extended springer front end, not only pays tribute to Mann's painting; it pays tribute to the man to whom Mann's painting paid tribute: one of Mann's fallen brothers named Cannibal Willy.

YOUNG BLOOD, OLD IRON

Most bikers love Mexican food and margaritas and that is exactly why the first meeting for a new magazine dedicated to the new breed of young riders was held at the Latigo Kid restaurant in Agoura Hills, California, just blocks from *Easyriders'* corporate offices. The soon-to-be editor of this fledgling rag, Cary Brobeck, roared up to the cantina on his oil-dripping Panhead chopper and came in carrying young gun gold: back issues of *Easyriders* from the 1970s.

The riding world was poised and ready for the new magazine that we decided to call *WRENCH* (which debuted in November 2012). When creating the parameters of *Easyriders'* newest biker magazine, Cary and I spent many hours pouring over back issues of *Easyriders* to define exactly what these new guys like and what they don't like when it comes to the biker lifestyle and what it represents. Fueled with a fierce passion for the true origins of bikerdom and Cadillac margaritas, we envisioned a magazine that captures the fun and attitude of riding impractical choppers, camping on top of scorpion nests, and catching venereal diseases, but not being able to remember the fun we had the night before.

As part of his research, Cary volunteered to visit a slew of bike shops and drink them out of their Pabst Blue Ribbon, ride with absolute madmen to places

OPPOSITE: Sherm shows off his "bars to the stars" ape hangers. Love the turned lowers.

without names and delve into the rampant debauchery, and ride on every half-worthy motorcycle run and rally in the land to siphon the essence of young blood bikers and pour it into the very ink of the words he writes.

WRENCH would feature the custom motorcycles that our readers ride, or hope to build and ride. These riders don't want to just buy a stock flat-black Sportster or Dyna from their Harley dealer and ride around pretending to be Sons of Anarchy. They want vintage-style choppers with beating hearts made from old iron.

You start with a rigid frame. A vintage Harley frame is preferred. To make that frame a roller, you'll need a front end, wheels, and tires. For a real chopper, you'll want an extended springer front end. There are lots of choices for a minimalistic gas tank, like a stock Sportster peanut tank. But the jewel in the crown of any chopper is the motor, the beating heart of the beast. While the obvious choice and the favorite picks are vintage Harley motors such as Knuckleheads, Panheads, Shovelheads, and Sportster motors, many young builders looking to build a bike on the cheap also use motors from Honda

CB750s, Yamaha XS650s, and various old Triumphs and BSAs. Used Harley Evolution motors can also be had on the cheap; even an Evo is considered vintage today and Harley made hundreds of thousands of them.

Even though *Easyriders* focused on American iron, the magazine always included the occasional custom chopper with a Triumph motor cradled in its rigid frame. Many of the original one percenter clubs allowed bikes built by those countries that stood with us in World War II, while bikes built by our enemies were never allowed. That's why you never find a club member riding a Honda or BMW chopper. Custom Triumph choppers and bobbers have always been as cool as hell and today's bikers build some bitching examples. In 1946 Triumph began selling motorcycles in California, and the 650cc Thunderbird 6T model (made famous by Brando in *The Wild One*) was launched in 1949. The Thunderbird was designed to satisfy the power-hungry American market. By the mid-'70s, Triumph sales dropped and production was discontinued in 1983 when the firm went into liquidation. Triumph was reborn in 1990, and today the company is stronger than ever.

"EASY RIDER WAS
   NEVER A MOTORCYCLE
   MOVIE TO ME. A LOT
   OF IT WAS ABOUT
   POLITICALLY WHAT
   WAS GOING ON IN THE
   COUNTRY."
               —DENNIS HOPPER

Although one percenter clubs never allowed motorcycles from Axis powers, back in the '70s many crazy long choppers were built around Honda's CB750 four-cylinder motor. This air-cooled, transverse inline four motor debuted in 1969 and was considered the first superbike. The original single-cam engine stayed in production for ten years, with Honda producing a whopping four hundred thousand units. Within a few years, used bikes and motors started showing up on the cheap and custom builders began wedging them into rigid chopper frames. Chopper magazines in the mid-'70s, like *Street Chopper*, *Custom Chopper*, and Ed Roth's *Choppers Magazine*, were full of amazing choppers based around the Honda CB750 Four motor.

From the beginning, *WRENCH* magazine wanted to show readers the kind of events and custom motorcycles that captured their way of life. That premiere issue included a Flathead chopper with a girder front end, a 1978 Shovelhead chopper with a narrow glide, a 1968 Triumph Bonneville chopper, two crazy Honda CB750 Four choppers, another 1978 Shovel chop, and a 1975 Yamaha XS650 in a rigid frame. We also ran a story about how you could buy an entire rolling chassis kit to fit 1970–1984 XS650 motors. Although the price of Yamaha XS650 motors has started to climb, it's still a great way to build a chopper of your own when you're high on motorcycle passion but low on dough.

THE
SHOPS

♠

WHERE TODAY'S BIKERS HANG, DRINK BEER, AND WRENCH ON THEIR SCOOTS

Every biker should have a local shop to hang out with like-minded brothers. A shop not only functions as a motorcycle fabrication shop, but it's also the center of social activities, a part of the community. It is a place where young men learn to wrench on their scoots and learn how to be bikers, a place where you can drink beer and belch really loud. When motorcycles are your religion, it is your church.

I found such a shop when I was just fourteen years old, a small motorcycle repair shop in North Miami Beach, Florida, filled with an unusual mix of gypsy-like people and a wild assortment of motorcycles parked out front. The sound of laughter mixed with the clanging of wrenches and the occasional cacophony of a bike starting up, and sometimes music would drift out onto the street, anything from top-40 rock to bellowing opera.

Though small in size, Jason's garage is filled with old-school cool.

"BIKERS DON'T BECOME FRIENDS; THEY BECOME FAMILY."

—UNKNOWN

The place was wedged into an aging strip mall and was closed on Mondays, so I rode over on a Monday afternoon on a reconnaissance mission and took a look inside the glass front window. I noticed a few old motorcycles for sale near the window, a BSA Golden Flash, a Honda CB350, and some sort of ancient black. I later found out it was a 1959 BMW R50.

A dusty display case acted as the parts counter. A cash register dominated one end and beneath it, behind glass, were bizarre biker curio items such as a Rat Fink statue, various colors of Harley wing patches, biker wallets, and leather gloves. Leather jackets hung on the wall to the right, above a rack containing T-shirts bearing the legend: "Gunner's Cycles." The shop area in the back was a complete mystery from the front window. Through the black maw of the open door to the mechanic bays, I caught the merest glint of chrome handlebars. Looking up, I studied the stickers and metal signs along the top of the storefront's glass window: Moto Guzzi, Bosch Sparkplugs, Triumph Motorcycles, and the Harley-Davidson bar and shield.

After gleaning all the intel possibly from the front of the place, I rode my bike around back and was instantly hit with the smell of old motor oil and rancid beer. The back garage door was locked up tight, but there was a stack of ancient motorcycle tires, a big drum that I supposed was full of used oil, and another open-topped drum full of beer cans and cigarette butts. A handmade sign on the back door proclaimed: "Premises Protected by Thor!" Just as I wondered at the sign's meaning, I heard something big hit the other side of the roll-up and the unmistakable fierce barking of a guard dog. Thor, I presumed.

The feeling in my stomach was a mixture of fear and excitement. This was a place with a story to tell. I had discovered the gateway to the secret world of bikers.

Since it wouldn't be cool to ride up on a bicycle, I elicited the help of a friend who had a battered and bruised Vespa. After school, I got on the back of my friend's scooter and we rode over to check out Gunner's. David wore a World War II GI helmet and his brother's faded jungle camo jacket. As we parked the Vespa out in front of the shop, two guys were mounting up on their bikes. One was a Harley Sportster and the

OPPOSITE TOP: Aki Sakamoto opened his custom bike shop Hog Killers in 2009 in Hawaiian Gardens, California. FAR LEFT: Originally from Fukuoka, Japan, Aki has had a passion for motorcycles since he was just a kid. LEFT: All of Aki's Hog Killer parts are made in the United States.

OPPOSITE TOP: One of the prettiest Shovelheads ever seen. Aki has added his Hog Killers air cleaner cover and points cover. OPPOSITE: Hog Killers oil tanks offer a cool custom look.

other was a small Triumph. They kick-started their bikes and roared off into the blaring Florida sun, the embodiment of cool.

Eager to get inside, out of the heat, and see what two-wheeled wonders awaited, we rushed in and looked over the used bikes, drooling with pure motorcycle lust. Gunner himself was behind the counter, helping a customer who was buying some engine gaskets, looking like a Viking with his long red hair and beard. He laughed as the customer left. Then I realized that David and I were the only other humans left in the shop. Gunner called out, "Can I help you, fellas?" We hadn't prepared for this basic question; neither of us had given any thought to how we would respond to an interrogation.

My friend piped up, "How much do you want for this BMW?" And suddenly, we knew that we had found a second home. Gunner, who's full name was Gunther Ziegler, was more than happy to talk about motorcycles, even to two kids who obviously didn't have five bucks between them. That first afternoon we learned something of the history of BMW and their fine motorcycles. We also found out, in great detail, why Gunner had a firm belief that Bosch sparkplugs are the best in the world. We also met Thor, a big blue Doberman. Much like Gunner, Thor looked intimidating, but both man and dog turned out to be big sweethearts.

That summer, I worked at Gunner's for free, sweeping up, running to get Gunner and his mechanic lunch, stocking shelves, and learning as much as I could about how motorcycles work. After my birthday that summer, I got my restricted license, saved up, and bought a very used Honda 90. My mother hated motorcycles, but my dad helped me trade the Honda in for a used Harley Sprint at Christmas. It only had one cylinder, but it was black and had a Harley-Davidson badge on the tank! Gunner christened my Sprint by pouring beer all over the tank.

All bikers need a place like Gunner's to hang out, to talk motorcycles, and to fall in love with the lifestyle. It is with this in mind that I'd like to share with you some truly righteous shops. Each has its own vibe, but all are dedicated to the two-wheeled church of steel, grease, and gasoline.

HOG KILLERS

Aki Sakamoto is one of the most talented and yet also one of the most humble and friendliest custom bike builders in the country. He has a great

"WE ARE COMPLETE SOCIAL OUTCASTS—OUTSIDERS AGAINST SOCIETY. AND THAT'S THE WAY WE WANT IT TO BE."

—A HELLS ANGEL

Before opening Hog Killers, Aki worked with Jesse James at West Coast Choppers for a number of years.

"WHENEVER A BIG MOTORCYCLE SHOW WAS COMING UP THERE WOULD BE A LOT OF ACTIVITY TO GET THE LATEST CUSTOM BIKE READY FOR THE SHOW. DAD WOULD WORK ON THE BIKE RIGHT IN THE FRONT ROOM OF OUR HOUSE."

—CORY NESS, SON OF ARLEN NESS

eye for design, a true love of old iron and old-school choppers, and a wonderful sense of humor. He calls his shop Hog Killers because he takes big, fat, stock Harley hogs and trims them down to lean, mean choppers. Aki was Jesse James's top engine builder and ace mechanic at West Coast Choppers (WCC). After the TV chopper madness moved on to the exploits of the Kardashians, Aki opened Hog Killers.

Hog Killers does it all, from changing the oil to full-on ground-up custom builds. Hog Killers also offers its own brand of cool custom parts and accessories. The HK parts line is not some cheap, mass-produced, overseas crap; it's all proudly made in the USA.

Aki does all the wrenching, chopping, and fabricating with the help of a dude named Tetsu.

Contact Info

Hog Killers Inc.

562-276-3427

www.hogkillers.com

AT THE RISERS

Jason Webber's jeans have real dirt on them and his beanie smells worse than his beard. He works out of his garage in Anaheim, California, crafting classic bike builds, selling one-off parts and making At the Risers (ATR) trucker hats and T-shirts with Nick Simich. These hats and shirts are some of the coolest shit you can buy if you are into choppers. A certified electrician for twelve years, Jason has a job that allows him to have the best of both worlds. He can support his chopper habit and also support his wife and daughter.

Jason is a chopper hoarder. While some people collect *Star Wars* action figures, this biker has a collection of cycle nostalgia ranging from helmets to gas tanks, fenders to primary covers, and Pan to Shovel motors among the bikes residing on his homemade lifts.

Like many young gun builders, Jason has a lot of passions, being an electrician, bike builder, parts maker, hoarder of motorcycle stuff, and loving husband and father. And his true love is skating.

Contact Info
At the Risers
www.attherisers.bigcartel.com
www.attherisers.blogspot.com

ABOVE: Jason Webber's garage-based shop, At the Risers in Anaheim, California. RIGHT: Jason's motto for his company is "bikes from the past, breakin' down the future."

INDIAN LARRY MOTORCYCLES

Bobby and Elisa Seeger of Indian Larry Motorcycles are the nicest people in the world, and they've been through much grief, first with the passing of Larry in 2004, then with the passing of their son Aidan to adrenoleukodystrophy (ALD) in 2012.

Indian Larry Desmedt's shop Grease Monkey in Brooklyn was known for the mechanicalness of Larry's motorcycles. Larry liked to see every detail displayed. A simple motorcycle stunt called "the crucifix," which Larry had done a million times before, went wrong during the filming of an episode of Discovery Channel's *Great Biker Build-Off*. Larry fell backwards off the bike, hit his head on the pavement, and died. But the motorcycles that Larry loved live on in Indian Larry Motorcycles in New York. Bobby and Elisa Seeger still run the shop.

Contact Info

Indian Larry Motorcycles
718-609-9184
www.Indianlarry.com

THE CYCLE LODGE

The Cycle Lodge is a true motorcycle museum for chopper freaks featuring the work of a true kustom kulture artist, John "the Harpoon" Haprov. John spent his formative years honing his printing and painting skills inspired by friends and mentors Ed "Big Daddy" Roth and Larry Watson. Roth gave John the nickname "Harpoon." He picked up his first striping brush at the age of sixteen and eventually began painting entire bikes. These days he spends his spare time painting and printing posters and shirts for both his personal work and for Freedom Machinery and Accessories (FMA).

Harpoon and Grant Peterson run FMA out of the appointment-only Cycle Lodge in Orange, California. This is also where all of the bike building and shenanigans take place. You can find a veritable "who's who" of the Southern California motorcycle scene hangin' at the Cycle Lodge on any given night. You'll also find some of the rarest and most interesting parts and motorcycle-related memorabilia imaginable. The coolest part of the Cycle Lodge is the garage, where, amid collections of old bikes and usable parts, old choppers are built or worked, and maybe a little pinstriping by Harpoon takes place.

OPPOSITE: The three amigos have been collecting cycle stuff all their lives and finally have a place to display it all. **ABOVE:** The lodge is also the birthplace of the annual Born Free show and a place where Harpoon does his paint work.

Contact Info

www.choppedout.blogspot.com

www.freedommachineryacc.bigcartel.com

"ONLY BIKERS KNOW WHY A DOG STICKS HIS HEAD OUT OF A CAR WINDOW."

—UNKNOWN

SPITFIRE MOTORCYCLES

To see the best examples of meticulously hand-built custom choppers, look no further than Paul Cavallo's Spitfire Motorcycles. Paul grew up in his father's machine shop, working with some hardcore bikers. It wasn't the long gray beards or dirty vests that drew Paul to the biker lifestyle; it was the killer choppers they rode.

Paul used to hang around the old Harley dealership in Pomona known as "the brick yard," driving everyone nuts asking questions about bikes that he clearly couldn't afford. Since he couldn't buy a bike outright, he decided to hit the swap meets. He came upon a lot of beat-down, shitty old parts, and he got a world-class education in how to repair cracked and broken engine cases. He discovered a shop called Beck's Chopper Design and convinced Jim Beck that he was serious about building a bike. The crew at Beck's took Paul under their wings and taught him all sorts of stuff, like how to sweep the shop floor, pick up food, and run parts around. That shop became a second home to Paul. When Paul started making the parts he couldn't afford, some friends noticed and wanted Paul to make some for them as well. Paul dug into his dad's machine shop and started making a few parts to sell, just to fund another build down the road. The orders started rolling in pretty heavy so Paul started a parts company called American Made.

Eventually, Paul started Spitfire Motorcycles. His goal was simple: provide quality, American-produced parts at a price that people can afford. It's not easy to compete with companies that are importing their goods from Taiwan or China when you have the overhead of a manufacturing facility in California.

Paul Cavallo builds motorcycle parts because he loves motorcycles, and he can't see himself doing anything else. He can usually be found in his shop at all hours of the day and night.

Contact Info

Spitfire Motorcycles

www.spitfiremotorcycles.com

THE RABBIT HOLE

Robert Hernandez, the owner of the Rabbit Hole, a small shop in Phoenix, Arizona, has no website or business cards; he prefers old-fashioned word-of-mouth business. He is not looking for approval in his builds or for "likes" on Facebook. He looks forward to a time when choppers are no longer cool; he will still be building bikes because of a true love for old motorcycles, and not for a love of being cool.

Motorcycles are in Robert's blood. He got his start riding dirt bikes, and he learned to fix things from his grandfather. Fixing things is what Robert does best. The Rabbit Hole started with Robert working on his own bike and a few friends' bikes as a hobby. By 2007, he had started taking on some paid jobs. One year later, he was making a living building motors and bikes. He never intended for any of this to happen, so he never named the business. As a joke, he started calling it the Rabbit Hole and the name stuck.

Contact Info

Word of mouth only

OPPOSITE: Paul Cavallo opened Spitfire Motorcycles in the Inland Empire of Southern California in 1994. ABOVE LEFT: Paul is known for creating one-of-a-kind custom choppers, parts, and accessories. ABOVE TOP RIGHT: Check out the attention to detail on this generator lower end. ABOVE RIGHT: Paul is known for creating the unimaginable and fabricating the impossible.

This best-of-show winner made the cover of *Easyriders*.

BONES LEGACY

Paul Ponkow's shop, Bones Legacy in Las Vegas, Nevada, is as clean as a laboratory and packed with pristine examples of true old-school choppers. There's even a crazy, Ed Roth–looking contraption that rides on four dragster tires in back and a super long springer in front balanced on a nimble 21-inch front wheel.

One entire wall at Bones Legacy is dedicated to framed bike features and trophies that Paul has won for his amazing machines.

"My love of motorcycles started when I was a kid growing up in Wisconsin back in the 1970s," Ponkow says. "Wisconsin wasn't California, but it was the home of Harley-Davidson, and . . . there were a fair share of cool choppers around. Everybody had Schwinn Stingray bicycles, and when I got mine, I asked my father to cut the fork and add another one to it so I could have a chopped bicycle.

"My brother talked me into buying a 1970s-style chopped BSA with a H-D springer front end on it. I bought it and he rode it home. This was back when choppers were not fashionable and I was constantly pulled over by The Man.

"I started learning about bike building and customized the bike, but never put it into a show. All the British shops were closing and the old-timers were passing away, so I had to learn by myself. My brother passed away and for some reason I got this weird inspiration to go crazy and start entering the scoot in bike shows. Soon I was buying and restoring choppers and I always felt my brother was looking on and watching me.

"When I entered my first bike show in 1989, I met a bike builder named Bones for the first time and we hit it off. As time went on, he became my best friend and mentor. Bones was a true master builder. Bones passed away in early 2005. This is when I started a chopper shop called Bones Legacy with my friend Richie, in honor of Bones, to keep his legacy alive. Every bike I build has something on it that I learned from Bones. Richie and I have the same vision, passion, and love for these old choppers; we didn't just jump on the latest chopper bandwagon. We simply close our doors and focus on what we like to do, and reflect on the past with a little of our own twist."

Contact Info
Bones Legacy
www.boneslegacy.com

FOUR ACES CYCLES

One of the best British bike mechanics west of the Mississippi, Wes White, owns Four Aces Cycles, which specializes in British motorcycles. Wes has a true passion for all things on two wheels, especially Triumphs. He doesn't take on every project that comes through the door. He says that he's tired of taking $10,000 worth of parts and turning it into an $8,000 motorcycle.

Since 2006, Wes has been hitting the Bonneville Salt Flats trying to break some speed records. Two Midwest Triumph salt flat heroes named BIG D and Keith Martin have been mentoring him. If you have a Triumph in need of some fixing up and want it done right, look up Wes and his Four Aces Cycles.

Contact Info

Four Aces Cycles

818-834-1060

www.fouracescycles.com

www.4acesblog.blogspot.com

SPEEDMETAL CYCLES

Dave Barker's father was into driving and wrenching on race cars. Dave's dad still holds records at two dirt tracks. With this much fabrication and wrenching history in Dave's family, you could say he was destined to become a top-notch fabricator himself. It's in his blood. Dave knew how to weld before he was ten years old and would modify anything he could get his hands on. He started SpeedMetal Cycles in Denver, Colorado, sometime in 2006, as a way to make a few bucks in between tours with his band. Today, SpeedMetal Cycles is recognized as one of the top shops in Colorado.

The shop does custom bike builds from the ground up and also tackles lots of vintage Harley-Davidson restorations. Choppers are not a passing fad for Dave. He has fully emerged himself in the lifestyle. It's what he does and who he is.

Contact Info

SpeedMetal Cycles

www.speedmetalcycles.blogspot.com

Everywhere you look, you
see evidence of a lifetime
love affair with choppers.

OLD GOLD GARAGE

Dan Collins, a Southern California tattoo artist and fabricator of hot rods and choppers, opened Old Gold Garage around thirteen years ago. He started working when he was fourteen years old so he could buy his first car. "I wanted an old Trans Am or a 1967 Camaro, but those were out of my league at the time. I ended up with a cherry '70 Firebird that I drove to high school my junior year," he says. "I also bought my first Harley that year. It was an almost stock Ironhead Sportster. I had them both painted black, but other than that, I left them mostly stock.

"Around 1990, some dude in Sun Valley where I worked owed me some money. He didn't have it, so in trade I got an old neon Budweiser sign and an extremely haggard, old MIG welder. The bike scene back then was nowhere. Hollywood was filled with glam rockers riding cherried-out full dressers and Softails with neon paint jobs. It was the beginning of the Rubbie era. Lawyers and doctors were buying Fat Boys and chaps and playing dress-up on the weekends.

"I started tattooing around the same time as I got into bikes. I grew up in Hollywood, left home at sixteen, and moved in with some guys in a local band. I worked a telemarketing job with the drummer and guitar player. One day I was flipping through some vinyl in a milk crate and found what turned out to be a homemade tattoo machine made from a Walkman motor, a Bic pen, and a guitar string. My roommate Drew told me to go buy a 9-volt battery and he would let me tattoo him. I was a pretty good artist for my age, and so I did my first tattoo on his kneecap. It was a goldfish. He convinced me then to order some professional gear out of the back of a magazine. It took me years before I was any good. But that was the start."

These days he owns Old Gold Garage, a shop that builds bikes and chopper products. Dan says, "My parts are a little more expensive than the Chinese stuff and might take a few days longer to get to your door,

"PATIENCE IS SOMETHING YOU ADMIRE IN THE DRIVER BEHIND YOU AND SCORN IN THE ONE AHEAD."

—MAC MCCLEARY

> **"THOSE EXTREME-SPORTS KIDS TODAY ARE GOOD, BUT THEY HAVE IT EASY. TRY FALLING OFF OF A MOTORCYCLE GOING SEVENTY OR EIGHTY MILES PER HOUR ON ASPHALT. BELIEVE ME, NOTHING EQUALS IT."**
>
> —EVEL KNIEVEL

but most of my customers appreciate the quality and soul that goes into them, and that's priceless."

He says he wouldn't trade his life right now for anything. "I'm not good at routine. Some days I'll stay home and paint or engrave, and other days I'll work a fourteen-hour day at the shop, and then on most Saturdays I can be found at Dolorosa Tattoo, although I just tattoo by appointment these days. Most people don't know what to make of that. They think you have to be a bike builder, or a tattoo artist, or a mechanic, or a painter. The truth is I'm just an artist that likes to work in many different mediums. It's as simple as that."

Contact Info

Old Gold Garage

805-644-1959

www.oldgoldgarageco.bigcartel.com

Thanks Gunner

The bike shops in this chapter represent just a smattering of the kinds of quality chopper builders, fabricators, painters, and parts makers that are keeping the love of old choppers alive in America today. There are hundreds of such shops all over the world manned by passionate, dedicated bikers. When devising the list, I started to wonder whatever happened to Gunther Ziegler and Gunner's Cycles. The strip mall where Gunner's had been is now long gone, replaced by a furniture store. Could Gunner have guessed that the boy he allowed to sweep up his shop and experiment with turning wrenches would grow up to be the editor of the world's biggest custom motorcycle magazine?

Thanks, brother.

5
THE
CHOPPERS

♠

EVERYTHING OLD IS
COOL AGAIN FOR THESE
OIL-DRIPPING BIKES

Bikers would not exist without the bikes they ride. A biker without a motorcycle is just tattooed trailer trash, a drinker of shitty beer. Take a biker off his bike and he looks totally out of place, your fuck-witted cousin trying to fit in at your stepmother's wedding. But let him kick start his fire-breathing chopper and damned if he isn't a god among men.

Choppers, like hot rod cars, have always been cool. The custom choppers of old, for instance—a typical rigid Panhead chopper, the hard-edged cool blue-collar bikes that you can ride the living shit out of—were purchased on the cheap, discovered in barns, covered in cobwebs, found in crates at swap meets, and sold as basket cases pulled from someone's basement.

Current custom trends have come full circle. Back in the 1960s and '70s, a typical chopper might be an oil-leaking,

Portrait of the American biker: Davey and his Pan/Shovel.

irritable, 750cc Royal Enfield twin in a stretched rigid frame with a sixteen over springer front end and a king and queen seat made out of faded blue jean material with the famous Zig Zag man embroidered on the backrest. Riding such a beast required dedication. There was no way to tell when the gas was running out other than that the motor started to die and the rider would have to switch the petcock over to reserve on the tiny peanut tank before a semi-truck ran him over. There was no speedometer to help gauge how many miles had been covered so the rider had to guess when he was about to be out of fuel. If the rider didn't hit the downstroke just right when kick-starting it, it would launch him over the ape hangers.

The kind of chopper that was the shit back in 1973 is exactly the same sort of bike that today's next-gen bikers prefer. Today's biker looks back at the old-school biker legends and realizes that no matter how cool they think they are, or what new motorcycle they think they've created, those guys did it all first.

Rebels and outlaws have to push the envelope well past the sticky part, and now it's the younger generation's turn. They have to express their rebellion with

"THE STORY OF THE HELLS ANGELS MOTORCYCLE CLUB IS THE STORY OF A VERY SELECT BROTHERHOOD OF MEN WHO WILL FIGHT AND DIE FOR EACH OTHER, NO MATTER WHAT THE CAUSE."

—SONNY BARGER, HELLS ANGEL

both their lifestyles and their machines. The motorcycles in this chapter represent the current trend in choppers. The following is a cross section of custom choppers, ridden by this new generation of outlaws.

BEAUTY AND THE BEAST

Beauty and the Beast are two choppers started out on the same assembly line and ended up looking completely different. Anthony Calvillo and Ben Zales, the photographer for this book, each bought old, stock Honda CB750 Fours, but neither knew much about building bikes. Fortunately, they had a few friends who were willing to help out. Both of these bikes reflect their riders. Ben is a clean-cut biker, while Anthony is more of a greasy, bearded, dirty biker. From the start, Anthony didn't care much about fancy paint and shiny bits

OPPOSITE: Orange metalflake paint with lace details on Ben's CB750 tank. This look was all the rage in the 1970s and it's back! BELOW: Ben's super clean CB750 motor.

Ben and Anthony's Honda CB750 choppers show two different types of chopper builds—the garage build and the show bike.

"NEVER TRADE THE THRILLS OF LIVING FOR THE SECURITY OF EXISTENCE."

—UNKNOWN

and pieces. He just wanted to ride, and his Honda is as reliable as hell. While the Harleys in the pack usually have to pull over several times to bolt back on bits and pieces that have vibrated loose, Anthony's chopper just keeps rolling down the road.

Ben also intended to build a bike to ride, not for show, but he has gone in a slightly different direction from Anthony's black Beast. With custom pipes and the crazy front end, Ben went for the clean, classic look of a CB750 chopper that might have graced the pages of *Custom Choppers* magazine.

DEVILINA

Rather than building a custom chopper from scratch, a lot of people buy, barter for, or inherit choppers along with their idiosyncrasies and problems. Two New York One Percenters constructed *The Devilina* in 1974 as a tribute to the Devilina comic character (sort of a devilish version of Vampira). After completion, the club brothers found the machine to be untamable and outright dangerous to ride. The next owner rode the monster just a few times before pulling the original 1953 Panhead motor out, putting it into another bike, and stored *Devilina* in a barn, where she collected cobwebs. Some thirty-two years passed before Ryan Grossman, owner of Vintage Dreams Cycles in Los Angeles, got wind of the motor-less monster. A deal was made and *Devilina* traveled to the West Coast.

Soon after *Devilina* was at the shop, Ryan received news that his pal A. R. was on his deathbed from cancer. Grossman dropped everything and drove twenty-two hours non-stop to be with his friend for his last few days in this world. While Ryan and A. R. shared their last moments together, Ryan told his dying friend, "When you die, you're going to come back to life as a 1948 Panhead." In one of his last acts on earth, A. R. gave Ryan the motor and transmission that now give *Devilina* life.

TOP LEFT: Devilina's old, cracked survivor tank art. TOP RIGHT: A one-of-a-kind cross stoplight. MIDDLE LEFT: Look at that tank and neck. That's a lot of molding! BOTTOM LEFT: Ryan's ultimate 1970s barn-find, The Devilina, seen in his chopper warehouse on Skid Row in L.A. BOTTOM RIGHT: The molding and mural work goes all the way to the back fender.

Ryan brings *Devilina* to life with a few kicks.

DAVEY AND GOLIATH

Davey Copperwasher of Echo Park, California, learned about the pain and glory of bike building through an old Triumph with plenty of problems. He eventually traded his old British companion for some American iron in the form of a 1953 Harley-Davidson basket case. The motor cases, one of which was a 1953 and the other a 1949, were damaged so Davey had them repaired. The 1964 frame was turned into a sleek, rigid frame. Careful parts hunting and gathering, and hours and hours of studying the meaning of "Chopper," kept Davey focused and busy. After seven long months of having no running bike, the bike was assembled, welded, taped, and glued together to make one mean, and very shiny shovelhead chopper.

OPPOSITE TOP: Davey cranks it on, cruising through Echo Park, California. OPPOSITE: Davey kicking over his chrome Pan/Shovel in Silverlake, California. BELOW: Close-up of Davey's Pan motor with Shovelhead tops.

"I AM A REALIST IN ALL ASPECTS OF LIFE. I REFUSE TO ACCEPT SOCIETY'S SET OF STANDARDS, OR MORALITY. AS A ONE PERCENTER, WE BUILD A WORLD OF OUR OWN THAT VERY FEW CAN GRASP."

—BREEZE, ONE PERCENTER

A beauty shot of
Davey's Pan/Shovel.

THE PERFECT PAN

Jay Hollis always wanted a Panhead. He chased parts at local swap meets, traded with his pals, and made what he could in his garage. Slowly but surely, he created the bike he imagined. Not long after the Panhead was completed, Jay blew the motor up, leading to a fresh motor rebuild, and the Panhead has been on the road ever since.

ABOVE: Jamal's Panhead, a steel pony seen in downtown L.A. OPPOSITE TOP: The open primary side in all its glory. OPPOSITE: Jamal tuning the tricky Linkert carb on his Panhead.

HOBBS' HOG

When Eric Hobbs of Los Angeles brought his Panhead home, he was armed
with a weathered Harley manual for the 1954 FL. Hobbs had searched high
and low for the right Harley after selling his pimped-out Triumph 650. His
search finally led him to Lake Superior, Wisconsin, where he found the bike
that would become his chopper. Hobbs saw potential in the Panhead.

He soon faced his first obstacle after only two days of riding. A broken
motor mount meant he would have to pull the motor out of the frame and
give the bike a makeover. Eric got busy and put the motor in a rigid frame.
He ended up splitting the cases and trying his luck at a full engine rebuild.
Hobbs reassembled the motor with the use of his H-D manual. Hearing his
newly resurrected motor roar was the inspiration he needed to get the rest
of the chopper put together.

ABOVE: Eric's Panhead motor. OPPOSITE: Riding the hallowed highways of Los Angeles.

CHOP SUEY

Curtis Sorensen of Venice, California, started this project back in 2009. He built and then tore down this bike three separate times until it was finally done. He bought it as a basket case off of a drunk guy in Calabasas, California. It was half put together; the other half was in a couple of boxes. He rebuilt the bike, rode it around, decided he didn't like something, then tore it apart and build it back up. It was a cycle of ride, rebuild, repeat until he finally got the bike totally dialed in and named it *Chop Suey*. He's been riding the piss out of it ever since.

OPPOSITE: Curtis' Honda CB750 chopper in Venice Beach, California. ABOVE: A rigid frame, extended springer front end, pullback bars, a coffin tank, and king and queen seat just screams 1970s chopper.

CHATTY'S '55

Chatty always had a plan for a Pan. Originally, he wanted to piece one together by starting with a frame, then a motor and transmission, finally hitting up the swap meets and friends for whatever else he needed. But then Chatty realized his buddy Larry Nicassio had a nearly all-original 1955 Panhead in his garage. At the same time, Chatty was sitting on a fat stack of hundreds, so he decided to make Larry an offer for the Pan.

It wasn't easy, but Chatty and Larry put the bike together within a few months. It was probably not the best idea to do a shakedown run to Mexico and back, but Chatty decided to roll the dice anyway. His bike had some issues, but it ran the whole way and he was able to make it back home. The chop was popping, snapping, coughing, and leaking out of all crevices of the motor, but Chatty was still stoked on his bike and kept riding it all over the place. A few weeks later, his motor seized while doing 75 miles per hour on the 101 Freeway. His rear wheel locked up, and he had to skid over two lanes to get off the freeway. Although he almost died and crapped his skinny jeans, he was more bummed by the fact that his motor was burned.

Chatty pulled the motor and learned the piston rods had snapped and chunks of the cases were missing. Two months later, Chatty got his fully rebuilt motor back, and it runs like a top. Breakdowns and blowups are all part of the chopper experience.

OPPOSITE: Chatty and *Sally* kickin' it at the iconic L.A. River. BELOW: Chatty stops for a slice of pizza at Pizzanista.

"LIFE SHOULD NOT BE A JOURNEY TO THE GRAVE WITH THE INTENTION OF ARRIVING SAFELY IN A PRETTY AND WELL-PRESERVED BODY, BUT RATHER TO SKID IN BROADSIDE, IN A CLOUD OF SMOKE, THOROUGHLY USED UP, TOTALLY WORN OUT, AND LOUDLY PROCLAIMING, 'WOW! WHAT A RIDE!'"

—HUNTER S. THOMPSON

Ripping around downtown with a hitchhiker on the cobra seat.

WHITE LIGHT, WHITE HEAT

Luke McMasters of Big Bear City, California, found this beautiful first-year Shovel on Craigslist, in a misspelled ad that listed it as a: "1966 Harey Davidson." It was a first year Shovelhead with a 1956 straight-leg frame, a ratchet top transmission, and star hub wheels on a Wide Glide front end. Except for the tin, everything was good, including the price. Arriving at the house, he was greeted by three, bald-headed teens in khakis, chucks, wife beaters, and black and gray tattoos. The bald dudes introduced him to their dad, who was bench-pressing 220 pounds in reps of fifteen like it was easy. He looked at the bike, kicked the tires, checked the compression, and started it. Everything was good, so McMasters low-balled the shit out of the owner just to put him on his heels a little.

"Long story short," McMasters says, "we went back and forth and I walked away with a first year Shovel."

Over the next month, McMasters sold, traded, and bought parts for what would soon become the chopper he wanted.

OPPOSITE: This Shovel captures the essence of the chopper. ABOVE: Luke kicks over his Shoveled with a single kick.

Luke hanging out with
his nanny, Malice.

PENNSYLVANIA PAUL

Paul Luc of Pittsburgh, Pennsylvania, has an East Coast chop job, a 1955 Pan-Shovel, with West Coast roots. The chopper was originally built by Caleb Owens in Hollywood, California, then moved with its owner to Oakland and made it to Paul in Pittsburgh in 2011. It was Paul's first old Harley and taught him many lessons. He'd never owned a bike with a magneto before and he timed it wrong. "I must have kicked it one thousand times before I finally sought help," he said.

Since there's not a huge chopper scene in the Pittsburgh area, just a few guys around town share Paul's love for vintage iron, and they all help each other out.

BELOW: Paul Luc of Pittsburg, Pennsylvania, takes great pride in his CRO Customs 1955 Pan/Shovel.

THE RIGHT STUFF

In 2008 Ryan Cox went on a ride that included a guy on a 1948 Panhead. Ryan owned two Triumph choppers at the time, but he really wanted a Harley Panhead. Shortly after that ride, he heard that the guy he'd met was talking about selling his Panhead. So Ryan sold one of his Triumphs to gather some quick cash and gave the guy a call.

Ryan got the bike and changed everything but the frame and the front end; it still has the original 1948 wishbone frame and offset springer front end. The motor was pretty beat up so Ryan had it rebuilt. The heads were ported and polished with an Andrews A cam stuffed in there for good measure; now it's fast as hell and runs great.

"I had a specific vision of how I wanted the bike to look when it was finished," Ryan says. The transformation took four long years. He would do one thing at a time so that he could keep riding it in between fabrication. When he finally got around to having the tank and fender painted, he wanted something simple and understated. Ryan has always liked the look of the old Panhead police bikes, so he used that as the influence for the paint job.

BELOW: Ryan Cox rides the mean streets of downtown L.A. RIGHT: Ryan kicks over his gorgeous Panhead, a chopper version of a police bike.

ROOT BEER KNUCK

Sayer Cedillo of Reseda, California, grew up in a motorcycle family and has been around choppers his entire life. Both his parents are bikers, and Sayer was conceived somewhere in the Black Hills while his parents were on a trip to Sturgis aboard a 1950 Pan. With a motorcycle shop as his backyard playground and old biker movies playing in a continuous loop on the tube, he thought a chopped Knuckle made sense for daily transportation.

It took nearly ten years to build his vision of a true, traditional, 1960s-style Knuckle chopper. The bike is part of a family tradition; Sayer's father bought the 1937 Knucklehead motor years ago and had a big dream for building his own Knuck chopper. Many years later, the motor and plans were still on a shelf. When Sayer was only sixteen, he talked his dad into trading the Knuckle to

OPPOSITE: Sayer Cedillo grew up in a biker family in Reseda, California. His 1937 Knucklehead chopper is all about heart and soul. ABOVE: The devil is in the details. Look close and you'll find Rat Fink riding along with Sayer.

him for another bike and some parts his dad needed. About four years ago, he decided to finish the bike and have it on the road by his twenty-sixth birthday. The young biker did nearly everything himself; the paint and chrome were the only two things he didn't do. He rebuilt the motor and transmission and handled all of the fabrication work.

THE EMERALD DIGGER

This early Ironhead Sportster (1974) is a breed of custom known as a "digger."

Back in the '70s, Arlen Ness was known for building a style of custom bike that featured a spindly little stretched frame, minimal rear fender, solo seat, fairly stock length springer or girder front end, pull back handlebars and, most notably, a very thin, inverted, handmade gas tank that hugged the frame. Long, low, and lean, these digger bikes were all the rage in the San Francisco area and looked like a drag bike had married a chopper. Built for speed, they often used Sportster motors like the bike seen here.

Martin McLaughlin of Newport Beach, California, discovered this digger about three years ago while trolling Craigslist. The ad simply said: "1974 chopper." With no pictures or other info on the post, the two figured it could have been anything from a Shovelhead to an old Honda. Because the bike was located up north in Humboldt County, McLaughlin figured it might be something really cool.

The owner of the bike, a crazy hippie green farmer-type dude, told
McLaughlin over the phone that he had an old Arlen Ness digger with
an Ironhead drivetrain and a Ness Springer. On that info alone, Martin
agreed to send the guy $3,000, sight unseen. When he finally saw the bike,
he was a little bummed, but not shocked. It looked like some mid-'80s
monstrosity, complete with aftermarket billet wheels and a big tank. It
also had two flat tires, no electrics, and the whole thing was rattle-canned
cartoon purple. The bike sat in a corner for about a year until Martin and
his friend Machi ripped all the ugly shit off of the bike and turned it back
into a proper Ness digger.

OPPOSITE: Diggers
were made famous in
the 1970s by master
builder Arlen Ness.
ABOVE: Martin's build
partner Masaya Kosaka
sits on a true piece of
two-wheeled history,
a righteous 1974 Digger.

"YOU NEVER SEE A MOTORCYCLE PARKED IN FRONT OF A PSYCHIATRIST'S OFFICE."

—UNKNOWN

Snake of Los Angeles shows a little class by pullin' a full chopper wheelie on his 1955 Panhead.

SNAKE'S LONG BIKE

The story of Snake and his long bike begins with a biker hangout in Los Angeles call The Chun, which is both a place and a small collective of greasy motorcycle perverts dedicated to a life of discomfort, adventure, fun, and occasional projectile vomiting. Snake wasn't really into the long bike thing very much, but after sitting on *Devilina*, the long bike from earlier in this chapter, he decided that his next build would be a long bike.

He bought a Panhead, stared at it for a few months, but didn't know where to go next. He had absolutely no clue what the bike was going to look like. So, he did what any sensible biker would do—he got drunk and procrastinated. Eventually, someone brought over a 20-inch springer front end and Snake put it in the Panhead's frame. "It was the nudge that got me going in the right direction," Snake says. "After that, it all kind of just started coming together."

Snake learned a lot while building his long bike. All told, it took him about a year to complete his chopper.

"NOT EVERYONE IS GOING TO LIKE MY BIKES, JUST AS NOT EVERYONE IS GOING TO LIKE THE OTHER GUYS' BIKES. WHAT I DO IS TRY TO TREAT EVERYONE WITH RESPECT."

—EL PITTS, LAS VEGAS CITY CHOPPERS

"YOU HAVE GOT TO WANT TO BE AN ANGEL. WE DON'T JUST TAKE ANYBODY IN. WE WATCH 'EM. WE'VE GOT TO KNOW THEY'LL STICK TO OUR RULES."

—SONNY BARGER, HELLS ANGEL

6
RALLIES & RUNS

♠

BORN TO RUN AND SWORN TO FUN

Today's new breed of biker usually attends motorcycle runs and rallies created by like-minded young riders and the shops where they hang out. Many of these guys look down on the major bike rallies that take place each year across the country. They see mega rallies such as Daytona Beach Bike Week, Laconia, the Republic of Texas Rally, and Sturgis as parties for their granddaddies—overcrowded, overpriced events that are more like visiting Disneyland than being about and for real bikers.

But remember, the big rallies started out as small rallies started by guys who had a whole lot in common with riders today. For instance, the mighty Sturgis Motorcycle Rally that has been around since 1938. Today it attracts close to half a million riders to the little South Dakota cattle town each August, but it began as a weekend of racing put on by a few friends. Clarence "Pappy" Hoel owned the local

Jeremy and Ryan sailing through Death Valley looking like a scene out of the film *Easy Rider*.

Indian dealership and started a small motorcycle club known as the Jackpine Gypsies in 1936. They bought some cheap land and created a half-mile dirt track and hillclimb for racing their bikes. They called their meet the Black Hills Motor Classic and the first rally in 1938 only drew nineteen participants. In fact, the rally was so small that for the first few years, Pappy's wife Pearl made sandwiches for everybody and they all camped in the Hoel's backyard.

By 1950, the rally drew 388 riders. In fact, the Black Hills Motor Classic didn't really grow very much until it started getting a lot of press in motorcycle magazines. Bikers read about the Sturgis rally, thought it sounded like a blast, and started showing up in August every year. In 1965, the rally became a five-day event, and by 1975 it grew to seven days and Main Street was blocked off and was for "motorcycles only" so that bikers could park there.

Back in the 1970s, the area had few hotels or motels, and bikers just camped out in the City Park for a dollar a night. The park was soon overcrowded with beer-drinking degenerates who loved making noise and tearing around on their choppers.

OPPOSITE: Webber heading into Death Valley for the annual Death Valley Run. ABOVE: Ben and Ryan love long front ends; they just scream rebellion. LEFT: Jeremy "Raddy" Radford performs a gas station stop on-the-fly tune-up. BELOW LEFT: Eddie having his morning beer after a night of camping in Panamint Springs, Death Valley. BELOW: Pullbacks Forever, Forever Pullbacks. Ben takes a shot from behind his bars in Death Valley.

The City of Sturgis put up with these antics until 1976. Early Friday night of bike week, a rumor began circulating of a near-riot at Sturgis City Park. Meade County Sheriff John Egger's estimate of a half-dozen people arrested for "making trouble" was a little conservative. The picture changed dramatically in the next thirty-six hours when 104 arrests were made. Activity accelerated around 10 p.m. Saturday when bikers lit fires on the highway between the City Park and the Lions Club Park, then drag raced through the flames. Egger said his mistake was riding through the park between 10:30 and 11 p.m. that evening and via a public address system announcing: "We are going to wet things down."

According to Sheriff Egger, "Bikers responded with remarks such as, 'Hey, man, we'll get a bath!' They really started racing up and down the road then." The situation in and around City Park escalated each year until 1982, which the locals call, 'the year the rally almost ended.'"

LEFT: Snake waking up in a desert paradise after a night under the stars. ABOVE: Nick opens up his kicker cover at a gas station somewhere in Death Valley National Park.

ABOVE; Cary getting his El Diablo Run tattoo in Temecula, California, before riding down south into Mexico. OPPOSITE: Panheads like to be tuned . . . especially on the side of the road.

Due to rowdy behavior, the number of campers allowed to stay at the City Park was capped at 2,500. The rates were increased from $2 to $4 per night; this caused many to take refuge elsewhere and call for a boycott of the park. Campers were required to register, produce a license number, and abide by the city's "no visitors" regulation.

In addition, the park was divided into two sections to cut down on drag racing. Gates in the divider fence were torn down and rocks were thrown at city employees trying to fix the gates. Some of the campers used guns to threaten a backhoe operator and after that other city employees were threatened. That Wednesday, Sturgis Mayor Robert Voorhees ordered all employees out of the park. Bikers set fire to twenty of the porta potties in the park, tore out speed bumps, and chopped down a pair of trees.

Angry residents circulated a petition to end the rally and settled for not allowing bikers to ever use City Park for camping again. However, as the rally

"THERE IS NO SUCH THING AS ONE OF OUR BROTHERS IMPOSING ON ANOTHER."

—BREEZE, ONE PERCENTER

Miles of smiles and the occasional mirage on the El Diablo Run.

continued to grow in size every year, this led bikers to camp at now famous campgrounds outside of town such as the Buffalo Chip.

Chopper magazines such as *Easyriders* ran coverage of this big biker party every year and that made even more bikers take the ride to the Black Hills. By 1988, half of all bikers at the rally said they were there for the first time and attendance soared to 60,000 people. Infamous one percenter motorcycle clubs,

including the Hells Angels, Bandidos, Sons of Silence, and the Outlaws, converged on Sturgis for the fiftieth rally in 1990 and attendance is said to have been more than 275,000 bikers, who came from all over the world to be part of biker history.

When he and a few friends got together to raise a little hell and ride their motorcycles back in 1938, Pappy Hoel (who passed away in 1989) probably had no idea that his little event would turn into the monster rally it is today.

PREVIOUS PAGES: Strip clubs and tacos in San Felipe are an El Diablo tradition. ABOVE: Ryan helping a brother fix his broken Invader wheel in Mexico. Good thing someone brought a welder. OPPOSITE Palapas in the El Diablo San Felipe camp.

At the seventy-fifth running of the Sturgis Rally in 2015, attendance was estimated at 739,000 riders. The South Dakota Department of Revenue reported a record $413,763 in sales taxes collected within the city limits during the rally.

All runs and rallies start small, a few friends getting together and riding someplace or to putting on a little bike show in a park.

I've asked some riding buddies to help fill in the details for a number of the runs and rallies in this chapter.

TROY'S 666 DEATH VALLEY RUN

By Manboywolf (Adam Perez)

It was a perfect morning in Antelope Valley, off Highway 14, not a cloud in sight.

The diner about an hour north of Los Angeles was serving its customers warm coffee and cold eggs as six greasy choppers rumbled up. The riders entered the diner looking for caffeine and protein. Four more bikes entered the parking lot, then another group of six, until the diner looked like a small-time chop shop.

Finally, twenty-six dirty, rowdy bikers feasted and laughed inside the diner. The riders were having their second annual ride to Death Valley and Las Vegas from Los Angeles. A biker known as Uncle Troy, who first put the ride together, figured out the trip was a total of 666 miles; hence the name for the run.

The group finished eating and jumped back on the highway headed toward Death Valley, twenty-six loud and fast choppers filling the two-lane highway. With only one breakdown and one flat tire, the group made its way

"**THEY'RE THE WILD BILL HICKOKS, THE BILLY THE KIDS—THEY'RE THE LAST AMERICAN HEROES WE HAVE, MAN!**"

—ED "BIG DADDY" ROTH, 1965, SPEAKING ABOUT THE HELLS ANGELS

through the canyons and set up camp in the heart of Death Valley. Desert locals brought cases of beer and firewood throughout the night and the party didn't stop.

Once the sun rose, it took several hours to prepare the group for the stretch of riding out of the valley toward Sin City, but once the bikes were fueled and started, the ride was ready to move. Although Death Valley lived up to its name and claimed one of the rider's Shovelheads, they pressed on and made the trip to Vegas by nightfall. The band of bikers hit Freemont Street in downtown Vegas and drank with Sin City's best and worst.

The next morning the group divided up and headed home in smaller packs. Everyone was safe, breakdowns happened, money was won and lost, and the good times kept rolling.

OPPOSITE TOP: A rider prepares to ride his chopper on the dirt track. OPPOSITE: "Run what ya brung" dirt-track racing! ABOVE: Sumo meets Thunderdome in the "Cocktagon." Last man standing wins Biltwell prizes!

"RACING IS LIFE. ANYTHING BEFORE OR AFTER IS JUST WAITING."

—STEVE MCQUEEN

The line-up for the
EDR dirt-track races.

"YOU DON'T NEED A
THERAPIST IF YOU OWN
A MOTORCYCLE, ANY
KIND OF MOTORCYCLE."

—DAN AYKROYD

A trip with a 666 miles total has to have its demons, and although everyone made it back to their garages, the ride still sent four bikes home on the back of a truck. With bitching bikes, plenty of beer, and open roads, Uncle Troy's 666 Ride will be talked about all year long.

ROSARITO TOY RUN

By Cary Brobeck

For the tenth year in a row, Martin Resendez and his Rolling Deep 4 Charities brothers made a run to the border for the annual Rosarito Beach Harley Run. The run has become one of Southern California's premier biker charity events and has grown every year. This year's launch location was Laidlaw's Harley-Davidson in Baldwin Park. Several hundred bikers gathered on an early Friday morning to have coffee, donuts, and share a few laughs before hitting the road to the US/Mexico

OPPOSITE TOP: A long Ironhead chop rides through Born Free to enter the bike show. OPPOSITE LEFT: Raddy proves that Born Free is the place for the Three Bs: bikes, babes, and beer! OPPOSITE RIGHT: Ashmore and Jenny prove what you already knew: Girls LOVE motorcycles! ABOVE: A group of modern bikers at Born Free, taking it all in. This Orange, California, custom bike show and party is one of the biggest biker happenings around.

border. The first stop was Quaid Harley-Davidson in Temecula, where they picked up more riders, a quick bite to eat, and some fuel before heading to the next stop, Sweetwater Harley-Davidson in San Diego, just a few miles from the border.

After refreshments, the group started to line up and get ready to cross the border into Baja and meet up with the police escort to Rosarito. We estimated between five hundred to six hundred bikes on that first day alone. With another crew headed out Saturday morning, the total number of bikes had to easily hit seven hundred.

Once we crossed the Mexican border, a dozen or so Federales were waiting to help us get through the congested Tijuana traffic and onto the scenic toll road that leads to Rosarito Beach. This year's commute to Rosarito was a little different from previous years because the shorter and more scenic toll road was the route in lieu of the free central Tijuana roads. With the exception of the tollbooth, the ride was a nonstop beautiful coastal ride into town and to the doorstep of Papas & Beer restaurant and bar.

Once parked and inside Papas & Beer, things got interesting. What else would you expect from a bar with a swimming pool, a mechanical bull, sand, and never-ending buckets of Mexico's finest beer? Papas & Beer's wet T-shirt

contest is a great way to see your friend's wife naked. As night fell, so did everybody's guard. We ended up in some strip club, then almost in the back of a cop car, but all ended well.

The next day, the Rolling Deep 4 Charities crew started gathering about 11 a.m. to get ready to do what they all came for: help hundreds of underprivileged Rosarito children with school supplies, hygiene products, bicycles, toys, and clothing. This is truly the most rewarding aspect of the entire event, and the real reason why all these bikers make the journey into Baja.

Hundreds of kids gather with the help of Desarrollo Integral de la Familia (DIF), a Mexican organization that supports children's charities to distribute toys and other goods. The black T-shirt clad army formed a chain gang and quickly got out all the goods to the different tables that were set up by gender and age. Every box that came out of the overstuffed trailers was marked accordingly and sent down the line. When all was said and done, hundreds of kids went home happy, and hundreds of bikers went back to Papas & Beer to celebrate making a positive difference.

If you're interested in donating to the cause or would like more information on next year's wild ride to Baja, check out www.rollingdeep4charities.com.

MAMA TRIED

By Michael Lichter

Mama tried to raise me better, but her pleading I denied,
That leaves only me to blame 'cause Mama tried . . .
—From the lyrics to "Mama Tried" by Merle Haggard, 1968

So let me get this straight—a couple of guys decide to stage a first-ever grassroots bike show in Milwaukee in the middle of a very cold and snowy winter with just eight weeks to organize it? With the likes of old-school bike builder Warren J. Heir Jr. (JR's Cycle Products) and race-connected "Rockerbox" producer Scott Johnson behind it, anything is possible.

Scott approached Warren on several occasions about creating a grassroots show, but Warren always answered, "I fucking hate bike shows!" Then last December, realizing that they could control what bikes got invited to create a very cool show reflecting their vision, Warren relented and work began on Mama Tried.

With the help of the bike-riding hotelier Tim Dixon, who signed on his Iron Horse Hotel as an early show sponsor, the entire third floor of

OPPOSITE: A killer Knucklehead show bike at the Hippy Killer Hoedown. BELOW: Robert's very long Shovelhead chopper.

ABOVE: Busting balls and brotherhood at the Hippy Killer Hoedown. OPPOSITE: Adam's Shovelhead is sittin' pretty in Kutty's backyard.

the old candy factory located next to the hotel was made available. Invitations then went out to California builders like Scott "T-Bone" Jones, Denver Dan, Jeff Leighton, Will Thomas, Shawn Donahue, Scott Craig, Jeff Wright and Brad Smith from Iowa, Chicago's Brian Harlow, Josh Kurpius, Bobby the Leg, and Bobby Goodtimes, Minnesota's Dave Polgreen, Pete Mason, Jordan Dickinson, and Kevin "Teach" Bass, Detroit's Brad Richards, and the Haints from Alabama, with their off-the-charts energy. Everyone else seemed to fall in place.

Mama Tried opened Saturday morning at 11 a.m. and buzzed until closing at 11 p.m. Seventy bikes were on display despite wicked Midwest weather, ranging from highly polished Born Free invite bikes to greasy culture and racers right off the track. Paul Wideman (Bare Knuckle Choppers) hand fabricated every possible part on his spectacular new knucklehead and Ben "Bender" Boyle (Benderwerks) prepped his fat tire Pan/Shovel with 640 AMA-approved bolt-cutter screws for Sunday's spills and thrills on the ice. On the other end of the spectrum was Ray Bott's stock 1971 Shovel that he bought new. Warren, who personally invited Bott and his Shovel, told me: "Growing up in a Harley shop, this bike and Shovelheads in general resonate with me."

While Mama Tried was just a one-day show, with Saturday night's after-party at the Cactus Club, Sunday's ice racing on Lake Michigan, and all the partying along the way, it was quite a weekend for the six thousand–plus attendees.

www.mamatriedshow.com

BABES RIDE OUT

By Nina Kaplan and Celisse Muller

Wild women gathered from far and wide to ride to Borrego Springs, California. Our personal tripper witches congregated in Los Angeles the morning of the ride and caravanned out to the meetup spot. With our special ops Mama Alice at the wheel of the chase car and London's only JoJo in tow, the day started with a white-hot blast of energy.

I ended up arriving last and rode at the back of the pack until the frustration of following kittens on wheels through the rolling hills of Warner Springs was too much. We pushed forward into the wind—so far forward that we led the

"I REMEMBER THE FIRST TIME I SAW A HARLEY BOBBER BIKE AS IF IT WERE YESTERDAY. I WAS SEVEN YEARS OLD. A GROUP OF ROAD REBELS CAME ROARING UP AND I REMEMBER STARING UP AT THE BIG BIKERS AND THEIR BIKES. I KNEW RIGHT THEN THAT I WANTED TO BE A BIKER."

—MONDO PORRAS, DENVERS CHOPPERS

pack of women at the descent down Montezuma grade into the desert oasis of Borrego. The ride was golden. Upon pulling into town, we ate, drank, and loaded up the jukebox. Then we were gone to find our nesting spot by the mountains for the night.

We took a left turn at the corner where the gray paved road became two miles of off-white dirt. Whatever you do, don't use your front brake. I followed the path already created by the motorcycle in front of me. The setting sun cast a golden light on the surrounding hills while dust flew into my eyes. We finally made it to the dry lakebed that was our camp for the night.

A huge fire illuminated new and old faces. Night fell and whiskey flowed. The plan was to sleep out in spite of the discovery of several scorpions in the dirt. We shared stories, more than a few drinks, and enjoyed our renegade adventures at the dry desert lake. The rest was mostly a blur of boobs.

www.babesrideout.com

EL DIABLO RUN

Once again the boys at Biltwell Inc. put together another great biker run. Because of the abuse of the tequila and Tecate, I don't really know how many bikes were on the trip, but every year the same three hundred or four hundred people show up. Starting in Temecula and ending in San Felipe, Mexico, Biltwell provides a suggested route of two-lane roads, but riders are free to get there when and how they choose: no fascist road captains or mandatory riding formations. We had some minor issues with bikes that we had to fix on the side of the road that put us into camp a little late. The party was in full swing when we rolled in, hundreds of drunk dudes and chicks having the times of their lives, talking about all the mishaps and road beers they shared on the way in. Tequila and cold beers helped us catch up in no time.

After our late night of titties and tacos, the bikes firing up mid-morning rattled our eardrums. Hungover, we headed into town for some much-needed coffee and huevos rancheros. At breakfast riders decided if they would or would not enter the EDR Olympic Games that consist of a slow race, kick-start contest,

OPPOSITE: Eddie's kickass *Wheelie Machine*.

plank race and, of course, the infamous Circle of Death. In 2016 attendees were entertained by impromptu beach racing by a couple of inebriated bikers. It was a blast watching one bike get stuck in the sand and a brand new Harley-Davidson Breakout being launched straight into the Sea of Cortez.

The Master of Ceremonies McGoo did his best to move the motorcycle skill events right along and not make it an all-night ordeal. After all the events are done and the dust settles from the Circle of Death, trophies are handed out. Then the crowd moved over to the beach for the Cocktagon, something that could only be thought up by McGoo. Twenty-five men enter the Cocktagon, but just one man leaves. There is a giant cock and balls drawn in the sand, and twenty-five men buy whiffle ball bats for a winner-take-all fight to the death.

In the morning we mounted up and hit the pothole-riddled Mexican highway and headed across the peninsula. From the beaches of San Felipe to the mountains near Mikes Sky Ranch and back down to the beaches of Ensenada, there's some of the best riding with friends I have ever done.

www.eldiablorun.blogspot.com

BORN FREE

By Cary Brobeck

The Born Free bike show has become the biggest gathering of custom choppers on the planet in just a few short years. Grant Peterson and Mike Davis of the Cycle Lodge have turned a tiny California custom motorcycle event into a must attend for anybody on two wheels. People ride in from all over the continent and fly in from Europe, Japan, and South America. Most of the attendees either build their own bikes or at least heavily modified what they buy.

What makes this show so great is the amount of effort put into it all. Mike Davis and Grant Peterson work all year long to make sure the show stays the best. The formula is simple: handpick talented builders to build a bike.

Born Free has come a long way since the first gathering back in September 2009. A few hundred riders and onlookers, mostly local SoCal residents, made the trek that first afternoon. Born Free shows no signs of slowing down. The diverse crowd grows every year.

www.bornfreeshow.com

DAYTONA

Often a small run or rally will grow until it gets too big. Local police come in and demand the event organizers hire them to keep the peace and either charge so much that the event goes out of business, or the cops have such a high profile that it drives bikers away. The Laughlin River Run comes to mind. That run has never been the same since the shootout that happened between the Hells Angels and Mongols Motorcycle Clubs in 2002. The police presence is so over the top that it feels like there's one cop for every biker. As a result, nobody goes to it anymore.

This is not the case with Daytona. Along with the Sturgis Rally, Daytona Bike Week is one of the two biggest motorcycle rallies in the world, drawing hundreds of thousands of riders every year.

The annual Daytona run to the sun is often thought of as the first real rally of spring. Daytona is all about the pristine riding weather while the rest of the country is still digging out from the snow. While Sturgis and Daytona may represent the grandpa or weird old uncle to today's riding twenty-somethings, those runs are still part of the biker community.

Greg's killer Triumph chopper on display at Born Free.

7
LIVING
THE LIFE

♠

THE ATTITUDES, MORALS AND CODES OF CONDUCT FOR NEXT-GEN BIKERS WHO RESPECT OLD-SCHOOL ONE PERCENTERS

Today's youth need to be a part of a like-minded crew that they can bond with. They need to bond through rites of passage and a shared code to live by. This is often seen in urban street gangs and in motorcycle clubs. It is also seen in the relationship of the Wars Boys of *Mad Max: Fury Road*. There is a rich code of conduct to live by for these War Boys. Through constant acts of courage, valor, and devotion on Fury Road, they will die "chrome" and ascend to glorious Valhalla for all eternity. In other words, even in a post-apocalyptic world, a life filled with myth is a life filled with meaning and wonder.

Jeremy V. heads out on his home-built and painted Panhead in Highland Park, California.

ABOVE: Mark cruising his righteous Panhead through a scenic mining town, Julian, California. OPPOSITE: Seventeen-year-old young buck chopper head Joey and his Generator Shovelhead.

The bond between the War Boys is similar to the relationship that exists between members of a one percenter motorcycle club. In many ways, bikers live a larger-than-life existence. They create their own reality and find value in living a mythic life. Bikers are thought of as epic characters—sometimes cast as the villain, sometimes cast as knights on iron steeds. Often they are a mix of both good and bad, taking the role of the anti-hero. The biker has become an archetype in our society, and even when the concept of the modern-day one percenter has been delegated to the history books, they will live on in our imaginations and in the collective memory of humanity. As such, the biker culture will never die. The iconic one percenter will live as myth.

"SALVATION THROUGH FABRICATION!"

—JASON WILSON, SACRED STEEL

**"A ZEST FOR LIVING MUST INCLUDE
A WILLINGNESS TO DIE."**

—R. A. HEINLEIN, SCIENCE-FICTION WRITER

Many of today's new generation of bikers feel a real connection to the *Fury Road's* War Boys and the idea of finding glory and redemption out there on the highway. It is basically the same redemption that returning war vets found in stripped-down motorcycles in the 1940s and that a generation of dropouts and disenchanted youth found in the psychedelic choppers of the 1970s. As bikers of my generation used to say, the goal is to, "Live fast, die young, and leave a good-looking corpse."

There is a very real element of danger when piloting a motorcycle and that is actually part of the appeal of riding. The idea that death is riding on your shoulder and that your entire life is being balanced on a thin, 1-inch strip of rubber, is definitely part of the allure of blasting down the road.

Much like other transformative film franchises such as *Star Wars* and *The Matrix*, *Mad Max* tells the story of the hero's journey as mapped out by Joseph Campbell in his book, *The Hero with a Thousand Faces*.

When noting the similarities between the fictional motorized tribes in *Mad Max: Fury Road* to real life one percenters, we find many of the same elements of tribal structure, history, rules and regulations, and codes of honor. These are many of the same elements that make westerns and biker films so fascinating to watch. All present a skewed reality that we suppose is perhaps not that far from the truth.

In his book, *The Mammoth Book of Bikers*, author Arthur Veno supposes that many of the motorcycle clubs in Europe first defined themselves, their attitudes, and their custom bikes by watching American biker movies and adopting their very "bikerness" by imitating the actors onscreen. That's sort of like learning how to be a fighter pilot by watching *Top Gun*.

In researching this book, I interviewed a cross section of bikers, from the young-gun twenty-and-thirty-something, iPhone-toting, Shovelhead-riding pseudo hipster, to the forty- and fifty-something sons of old-school bikers, and even a few hardcore riding granddads in their sixties and seventies. These bikers run the gamut from mild ones to wild ones and come from every socio-economic strata,

OPPOSITE TOP LEFT: Camping in the horse stalls at Pioneer Town, California. OPPOSITE TOP RIGHT: Mark's ratty ol' Panhead chopper complete with weathered Bates seat. OPPOSITE BOTTOM: Knees in the breeze, Ben Zales kicks back on his chopper as he enters Joshua Tree National Park on Nash's Hell Ride.

"TRUE BROTHERHOOD IS THE KEY TO OUR SURVIVAL AND TO OUR WAY OF LIFE. WHAT MATTERS IS THE STRENGTH OF YOUR HEART AND THE LOVE OF YOUR BROTHERS."

—PSYCHO, ONE PERCENTER

every race, color, and creed. Trying to define a one percenter biker these days is a contradiction in terms. Members of outlaw clubs are often family men, and while they are rebels to the core, they also abide by the strict code of their clubs. While they are often loving husbands and fathers, they can also be violent when they feel their club or their brothers are threatened. But there are still basic lessons that are passed down to next-gen bikers, either by their own family members, by the members of the clubs they ride with, or simply by like-minded riders out there.

If your parents are bikers and you grow up in a biker household, one of two things usually happens: you either wind up as a biker yourself, or the values you learn keep you in good stead for a well-balanced and prosperous life. If, on the other hand, everything you know about bikers you learned by watching reruns of *Sons of Anarchy*, you could be in big trouble.

In all of these cases, however, there is a feeling that as bikers we have a real responsibility to teach the younger generation coming up the rules of the road. But what are these rules?

RULES OF THE ROAD

No matter who you are, what you ride, or who you hang with, the first and most important lesson to be learned is that of respect. Like most people, treat a biker with respect and you will get respect back. Act like an idiot and you could be asking for a good thumpin'.

OPPOSITE: At left, Bo's swingarm CB750 survivor chopper called *Stone Free*. BELOW: Ben on his way to the Salton Sea during Hell Ride.

Joey and his scoot.

"I FEEL LIKE YOU SHOULD BE DOING EXACTLY
WHAT YOU WANT TO IN LIFE, HOW YOU WANT TO
DO IT, WHEN YOU WANT TO DO IT. OTHERWISE,
YOU'RE WASTING YOUR LIFE."

—INDIAN LARRY

There is no reason to run and cower because some patch holders from the local chapter of some MC walk into the bar. If you are on a bike or part of a riding club, go on over (at the appropriate time) and introduce yourself, maybe even buy them a beer. If you are not a biker or on a bike, just leave them alone. You do, however, need to respect more than the one percenter himself. Respect his privacy, respect his colors, respect his bike, and definitely respect his woman. This may all sound like common sense, but you can never be too careful.

OPPOSITE: Shawn stopping for snacks at Tri-Co Shop in Hollywood, California. ABOVE: Will, one of the owners of Tri-Co Shop, offering cool T-shirts and chopper gear. The Tri-Co Shop is the physical store for *DICE* magazine.

A blog that is all about biker etiquette, www.bikerornot.com, has a list of rules that includes the following:

♠ If it's not YOUR bike, don't sit on it, or set anything down on top of it. That includes your lice-infested helmet, or the ass you haven't wiped for two days.

♠ Keep your dirty paws off my patch or my colors, my bike, my beer, and my woman.

♠ If you bump into me, more than a little, be quick with an apology.

♠ If you're a one percenter wearing a patch, live up to the dignity of the brotherhood; don't go starting fights in a bar. Why do you think the bars are banning colors? I'm tired of being confronted by punks who think a three-piece patch makes them more of a man than the low-life ignorant pissant they really are for starting a fight over stupid shit.

♠ **Road Rule No. 1:** Don't cut into the middle of a pack of riders for ANY REASON! If merging from or onto the freeway, slow down and fall in behind.

♠ **Road Rule No. 2:** Don't pass me in my own lane. Not only is it illegal, but I might accidentally stick out a boot and send you into the woods!

♠ **Road Rule No. 3:** If you don't know me, don't pull up beside me at a stoplight. I will automatically think you're up to no good and will react.

EVOLUTION AND REVOLUTION

One of the reasons that young bikers respect and honor older hardcore bikers is that by talking to bikers who have been riding for years, they receive knowledge of the road, of the trials and tribulations of building, maintaining, and riding a motorcycle. Older bikers teach valuable lessons regarding building secrets, they pass along the biker code of honor, and they tell great road stories. Plus, the young biker sees himself writ large in the weathered face of the older biker. Here is a man who has done it all, seen it all and lived to tell the tale. He is a man of honor, he is about

OPPOSITE: A rebel rider hot dogging on the streets of L.A. ABOVE: Brandon on his Cone Shovel, riding into the Born Free pre-party in Inglewood, California.

"IF I CALL YOU BROTHER, IT IS BECAUSE YOU HAVE EARNED MY RESPECT."

—UNKNOWN

"BURN RUBBER, NOT YOUR SOUL, BABY."

—CRAIG FERNANDEZ AND REGGIE BYTHEWOOD, *BIKER BOYZ*

something, and that earns respect of the deepest kind. After all, most young riders hope to someday become exactly that kind of dude.

If you ride, you know a brother who has fallen off his bike, or you yourself have fallen off your bike. Sometimes you fall, your bike gets damaged or destroyed, sometimes you get hurt, and sometimes you die. This unwritten code is the bond between bikers of all ages, but an old hardass always offers proof that you can live by the road and survive.

There has been enormous change in the biker community over the years. I think of the old Boozefighters as being full of fun, riding their bikes, getting drunk, and playing pranks on each other, and also being as tough as nails. I think of 1970s chopper riders as hippies on wheels, smoking dope, getting laid and popping wheelies on their laid-back long bikes. But the flip side of that flower-power coin was the hardcore one percenters who were happy to slap the taste out of your mouth if you looked at them the wrong way. Then the Rolex rubbie riders came along.

Now we can add the new cats on the block: vintage motor lovin' hipsters on leaky, old choppers who are out to have a good time and ride their machines without being hassled by the man. One of the things that every kind of biker has in common is a dislike for authority, a rebellious spirit, and a desire to cut their own path. They are nonconformists and a breed apart from the average citizen out there.

Several years ago I pitched the publisher of *Easyriders* an idea for a new magazine called *WRENCH* that would be aimed at the new riders that I saw popping up at bike shows, runs, and rallies. In order to define our audience, I had to do quite a bit of research on the demographics of these riders. The majority of *WRENCH* readers are male, a high percentage of them are college graduates or have had some college, and the sweet spot of their age range is twenty-four to thirty-nine.

OPPOSITE: The Chun Originals: Troy, Sean, Snake, Eddie, and Raddy in downtown L.A.

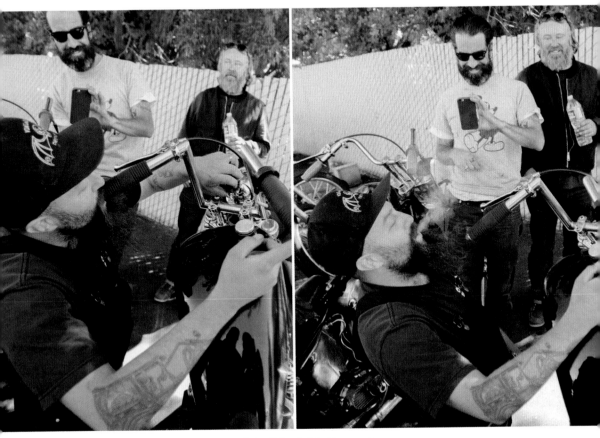

Ryan takes a hit on a custom-made handlebar that doubles as a pipe.

The new breed of bikers that I'm talking about seems to share certain attributes. Besides their genuine love of old iron, classic chopper styles, and riding the shit out of their bikes, they seem to be highly intelligent, focused, extremely creative and, though rebellious, very respectful. They are part of a generation that does not appear to have many of the prejudices and self-imposed limitations of my generation. They don't see color or nationality when they look at a person. They have fewer prejudices regarding sexual preferences, have a respect and reverence for the planet they are living on, and are kind to animals. They are often people with a purpose.

> **"IF I WEREN'T DOING WHAT I'M DOING TODAY... I'D BE TRAVELING AROUND THE WORLD ON A MOTORCYCLE."**
>
> —DONNA KARAN, DK FASHION DESIGNER

I find them to be confident and willing to fight the system. Many of the rules that my generation followed just seem silly to them and they fight them. They've evolved beyond the need for outmoded ideas and concepts. For that reason, old concepts of religious dogma seem archaic to them. They believe that pretty much everything worthwhile should be given creative thought. Everything should be questioned. As children, old control methods such as saying, "Wait until your father gets home," have no effect on them. They can also tend to be anti-social unless they are hanging with people who are on their same wavelength. They are big on brotherhood and integrity. And they are still bikers. They'll figure out a way to turn their Linkert carburetor into a bong, and if they run out of milk, they'll douse their corn flakes in Jack Daniels.

Like every generation of bikers that has gone before, the new kids don't want to be told what to do and what to think. And what happens when we refuse to "buy in" to the system that society pushes on us in order to be who we really are? For one thing, the conformists see us as nonconformists, as rebels and outlaws, and they would be right. Free-thinking individuals are every government's worst fear, the reason why society and the Bureau of Alcohol, Tobacco, Firearms, and Explosives thinks bikers have to be closely watched.

What the empty suits out there will never understand is that true freedom is found in living your life on your own terms. Circumstances may have influenced who you are, but you are completely responsible for who you become. All one percenters know this. Being a biker is about living the life you want to live, being the person you want to be, and attracting to you the things that you want in your life. The essence of the biker lifestyle, no matter which generation we belong to, is that each of us is allowed to be an individual and live as free men and women.

Free to ride.

8
THE RIDE NEVER ENDS

♠

THE CONTINUED NEED FOR REBELS IN OUR SOCIETY. A NEW GENERATION ANSWERS THE CALL.

The world will always need rebels to stir the caldron of convention. What follows is the true story one such rebel, of how far a man is willing to go to live the biker lifestyle and build an award-winning custom chopper from scratch. Thom Jones from Seattle, Washington, can tell you his story in his own words:

BIRTH OF A CHOPPER

This whole story started with an Instagram post I saw about three days too late. Ivan Snodgrass was selling a roller that he pulled out of a garage somewhere near Louisville, Kentucky, and was letting it loose to free up some room in his shop.

Al's super rad Panhead in Echo Park, Los Angeles.

From the photo of the rolling chassis, I could tell that the stance of the bike, with its long girder front end, was absolute perfection. You just don't see bikes with profiles that perfect every day and I had to have it.

I hit him up, we worked out a deal that we both could live with, and six months later, it wound up in front of my house with a shipper that delivered it on its side (that was a first). The bike sat in my garage for a couple of months as I didn't really plan on doing another bike for a year. But I just couldn't keep looking at it. With my current workload at the shop, it would be nearly impossible to build a Panhead motor, blast the frame, finish fabrication, get the frame shipped to my painter Denis, and have everything chromed in time to get it back to Seattle, Washington, assembled and ready for the 3,000-mile trip to Born Free in California and back.

To be straight, all of my previous bikes have been crusty, period-style bikes with minimal fabrication and tons of modified stock parts. The bulk of the work in those builds is in making everything look old, but with a show bike, I didn't even know where to start. I knew the frame had to be dealt with first because I needed to get it down to Denis at least six weeks before we left for the show.

"WHEN WE DO RIGHT, NO ONE REMEMBERS. WHEN WE DO WRONG, NO ONE FORGETS."

—SAYING ON AN OLD HELLS ANGEL BUSINESS CARD

I stripped all the paint and bondo off the frame to inspect the construction. After making a couple of small crack repairs in the lower tubes, I focused on the bondo restoration that would need to be done prior to shipping. I needed to change the handlebars, make a custom axle, finish the front brake mechanism, make a custom exhaust, make new foot controls/linkage, and so forth.

That bike sat in my workshop like an albatross that I had to walk around all day long, making it almost impossible to focus on anything but the bike itself. After several weeks, I managed to wrap up the fabrication enough to focus on the frame and tank specifically, which was the priority in order to get the bike to Denis. I spent the next two weeks doing nothing but bondo.

Once the rigid frame with its frenched-in gas tank and rear fender arrived in Southern California for paint, Denis began what I consider one of the greatest custom paint jobs in the history of motorcycles. Not only is it perfect for the bike, but it's absolutely perfect for the vision I had for this chopper. We shared photos daily of the progress, and as the whole thing unfolded before my eyes via iPhones from 1,200 miles apart, I began to see all of my show bike chopper dreams becoming a reality.

ABOVE: Derrek on the Death Valley Run with his knees in the breeze. OPPOSITE: Katy kicking over her Cone Shovel in Burbank, California.

The pressure was on to get the painted frame and tins back up to the rainy state of Washington. I still had ten days before I had to start the ride down to Born Free, and shipping was only two days in transit, so that left me eight days to get the chopper assembled and tested.

My plan was to assemble the 1963 Panhead motor while the frame was in transit. Two days went by, then three, and no frame arrived. I called the shipper only to discover that there was no active shipping record for the package and at that moment in time they had no idea where the crate was.

First off, when you have seven days to clear coat, assemble, wire, plumb, and shake down a bike for a 3,000-mile ride, you need every second of every day to ensure success. Finding out your shipper doesn't even know where the damned frame is sends even the most optimistic person into complete and total panic. I have a seven-year relationship with the shipping company, and I can assure you, that at the end of the conversation I had with them, they got an earful. Within three hours they had found the frame, sitting in an open air loading dock in sunny Los Angeles. I begged them to put it on a truck that had a two-man team capable of getting it to me in twenty-one hours.

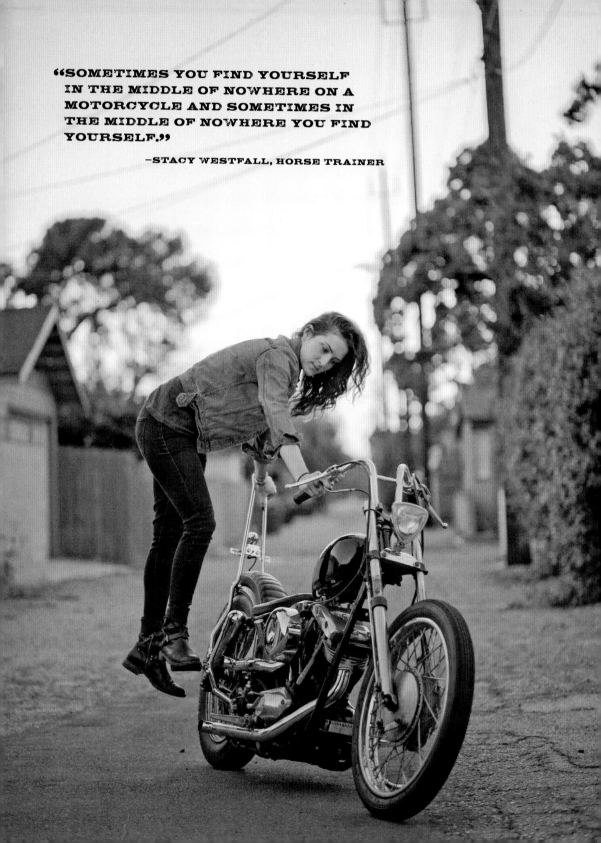

"SOMETIMES YOU FIND YOURSELF IN THE MIDDLE OF NOWHERE ON A MOTORCYCLE AND SOMETIMES IN THE MIDDLE OF NOWHERE YOU FIND YOURSELF."

—STACY WESTFALL, HORSE TRAINER

"WE CONDEMN ALL ONE-PERCENTERS. THEY'D BE CONDEMNED IF THEY RODE HORSES, MULES, SURFBOARDS, BICYCLES, OR SKATEBOARDS. REGRETFULLY, THEY PICKED MOTORCYCLES."

—AMA DIRECTOR, 1965, AMERICAN MOTORCYCLE ASSOCIATION

It was 4 a.m. when the truck pulled in to the terminal in Seattle and you better believe I was there, ready to throw it in my truck and race to my shop to lay down as many coats of clear coat as I could manage that morning prior to going about my regular work day.

I was finally ready to assemble the bike with just six days left prior to departure. As the motor and transmission were dropped into the frame that evening, my most pressing concern was whether or not my exhaust pipes, which were fabricated using a completely different motor and heads, were going to fit properly. Immediately upon mocking up the pipes to the mounts, it was clear that neither the front header nor the rear were going to fit. When you have perfect chrome pipes and you have to cut the flanges and reweld, you're fucked. The further I went down the rabbit hole of assembly, the more I realized that almost every part that was near that motor or those headers was now part of the domino effect of poor fitment.

I had just five days left before leaving for California and pretty much nothing was fitting. After another eight hours and two pots of coffee, things were starting to line up. My good buddy Jake Clifford came by that afternoon to document the project and was immediately handed some Mother's polish, a beer, and told to get to work. The two of us found a groove, and after a massive twelve-hour push, the bike was ready for wiring.

The next day I managed to stay focused and had the bike wired and ready to fire off around 3 p.m., with just four days left to shake it down. The bike fired right up, and after the third heat cycle, I was able to take her around the block. It was at that moment that I realized the challenge that a 30-inch over stock front end makes for navigating left and right turns, but she felt really good minus the hop in the rear brake. Convinced it was the drum, I replaced it and let the motor cool down for the big shakedown run in the morning.

OPPOSITE LEFT: Katy in downtown L.A. on her swingarm Shovelhead. OPPOSITE RIGHT: Sayer kicks over his show-quality Knucklehead. OPPOSITE: Ben's gorgeous Cone Shovel with "Prismic Style" Crazy Frank's fender, 20-over Harman girder, Hallcraft Satelite wheels, and Gary Little John space tank. All original pieces from the '70s.

Cary and Anthony in Phoenix, Arizona. There's no helmet law in Arizona and the boys look like Peter Fonda and Dennis Hopper.

"THERE IS A DELICATE RIDGE ONE MUST RIDE BETWEEN FEAR AND REASON ON A MOTORCYCLE—LEAN TOO FAR IN EITHER DIRECTION AND THERE WILL BE CONSEQUENCES."

—LILY BROOKS-DALTON, AUTHOR, *MOTORCYCLES I'VE LOVED*

"WHEN YOU'RE THE LEAD RIDER, DON'T SPIT."

—UNKNOWN

Overall, I was feeling really confident about the ride down to Born Free.

The next morning, I strapped a small tool bag to the sissybar and prepared to head down to my shop in the city. I really had no idea what it was going to be like, taking a rigid long bike on the freeways of Seattle, but I had three days to make sure this bike was going to make it to California and back, so it was time to make moves.

Whenever you pull out on a bike you have never ridden, your life sort of flashes before your eyes. An anxiety washes over you as you consider every single worst-case scenario in your mind. Are you going to stall at a light? Is the carburetor going to start popping and snorting? Are the brakes going to work? The list goes on and on.

On my 30-mile maiden voyage, I learned that the brakes on the bike were not operating properly. The front Invader wheel had a hop in it that needed to be sorted out and the vintage fuel petcocks were leaking gas all over the cylinder heads. I was lucky the bike didn't catch fire. Luckily, there was no explosion on the 15-mile trip back to the house, but the rear brake situation was getting worse by the minute. I pulled into my driveway, parked the bike, tore the front wheel off, and raced down to the fittings store to pick up parts for a couple of more "modern" petcocks, then headed straight to The WheelMaster to get that Invader sorted out.

On the final day before the long ride, I made sure all the nuts and bolts were locked down and packed up everything I thought I'd need for the trip. Four of us would be riding down to Born Free and we all needed a 2-gallon reserve of gas because there were a few places where no gas stations were for 150 miles and our small tanks only average 75 miles.

OPPOSITE TOP: Katy on her Shovelhead in Temecula, California. OPPOSITE LEFT: Gus rides through one of the many tunnels in Yosemite. Those pipes sure sound good in there! OPPOSITE RIGHT: Kevin on his too-cool Shovel in East L.A.

THE TRIP

We pulled out of my driveway by 9 a.m. the following morning. I was on a custom chopper that had less than 50 miles on a shakedown. The bike would have to run for the next two weeks and take me through six states.

Riding this motorcycle was unlike any other experience I had to date. When the only suspension on a bike is the air in the tires, you feel the road in ways that can leave you speechless, and not in a good way.

The bike was jetted perfectly as we headed up into the mountains and the plains of the high desert. By the end of the first day, we had ridden 420 miles, stopping in a little river town called John Day. We lost one of the guys in our group at the third gas stop so the group was down to three.

The next morning started with Jake being violently ill with a migraine, and as Dalen and I warmed up our bikes, we had concluded he wasn't going to be able to go any further. Amazingly, Jake managed to rally and we all headed out just after sunrise on day two.

ABOVE: Raddy lighting one up at the Newcomb Ranch biker bar in Angeles National Forest.
OPPOSITE: Rick looks like a righteous biker from back in the 1970s.

"IT WASN'T UNTIL I WENT TO COLLEGE AND I GOT MY FIRST MOTORCYCLE THAT I UNDERSTOOD THE THRILL OF SPEED."

—VIN DIESEL

The second day had a stop point in Reno, which was a little over 500 miles from John Day. With an earlier start and hopefully fewer issues, we would be able to make this trip with some time to spare and get to see the biggest little city in the world. Day two would prove to be one of the hardest days for me as the mountains' windy roads and 30-inch over stock show bikes don't get along so well. So a gorgeous ride through the mountains that would make most motorcycle enthusiasts smile from ear to ear just had me frustrated. With the hoppy brake, it was really hard not to imagine myself at the bottom of some canyon twisted up in a pile of candy paint and chrome.

ABOVE: Breakdowns happen. Loading up Austin's Knuckle that was acting up on the Death Valley Run. **OPPOSITE:** Shawn's camp in Death Valley. The perfect end to a perfect day of riding.

The sun was setting as we pulled in for the last gas stop of the day, ensuring that the last 60 miles of our trip would be in the dark and none of us had visible headlights (blocked by bags and gear). After filling up, we all shifted into first gear and started to head out, but when I stepped on my shifter, it just snapped right off, shearing through the bolt that held the linkage together.

We found ourselves riding into the busiest stretch of road we had traveled in 500 miles in the dark, and I had to shift my bike by pressing the edge of the linkage forward on a knife's edge, plus I basically had no brake. Not to mention that the cut on my lower back that was caused by the seat ensured that I was at a consistent six on the pain scale.

I was pretty convinced I was going to die, so I started planning ways to jump off the bike when that moment came. We managed to keep it together and got off at the exit that would take us to the Thunderbird Inn right in the heart of Reno's strip. As we pulled into this neat little slice of Reno's history, it became obvious that we would be the only ones staying at the motel that night, and when you ride up on three choppers, that's always a good thing.

We paid for the room, went down to the titty bar, and started smashing some much-needed cocktails. Jake had the great idea to shoot the bikes in front of the Reno sign, but I managed to lose my ignition key, so had to push the fucker down there and back to get the picture. We knew we had a long day ahead to get to my dad's place in Indio the next night. So we hit the hay with a healthy buzz, and a newfound respect for life, brakes, and headlights.

Day three began with what would become the most annoying aspect of riding the open-chain show bike, namely, adjusting the primary and drive chain. Each morning consisted of finding a parking block or rock to steady the bike on while this annoying series of adjustments took place. By the end of the trip, I was pouring so much Lucas Oil on the fucker that it was like having a wet primary. The left side of my shirt and pants looked like somebody just painted a brown line down my back.

"ANYBODY CAN JUMP A MOTORCYCLE. THE TROUBLE BEGINS WHEN YOU TRY TO LAND IT."

—EVEL KNIEVEL

"ON MY TOMBSTONE THEY WILL CARVE, 'IT NEVER GOT FAST ENOUGH FOR ME!'"

—HUNTER S. THOMPSON

The chain was almost completely stretched out as I had no adjustment left in the tranny plate and the drive chain was going to need about four links taken out. The situation wasn't ideal, but after the 580-mile trip we had in front of us for the day, I knew I could get it all sorted out after we got to my dad's. So with the chain slapping the frame and the shifter linkage now converted to a makeshift heel shifter, we hit the road on what would be the most difficult day of the trip.

At this point, the wound on my lower back had started to bleed through my pants. The pain was so intense that no position change or adjustment could alleviate it. Now mind you, I was the only one who knew about my injury at this point, because I was trying my best to keep a group of guys rolling. Plus the fact that we had what most would consider a near impossible distance to travel on some very old bikes.

By the second gas stop, we were warned by some travelers that Route 395 was closed due to the fires that never stop burning on the border of California and Nevada. We checked the road reports and decided to keep heading down the 395 instead of taking the bypass route and crossed our fingers that we wouldn't get turned around. We ended up making it through, and as we started the decent down from the high desert through Mono Lake, we began to see the most beautiful country yet on our journey.

OPPOSITE TOP: Tony's sweet Ironhead chopper. OPPOSITE: Noah waking up sometime in the afternoon after a night of partying. "Think I just blew about fifty bucks outta my nose just now!" ABOVE: The Death Valley Run Campsite at Panamint Springs.

For those of you who have never taken the 395 from Joshua Tree to Pendleton, I couldn't imagine a road more beautiful. I wouldn't recommend doing it on a full, rigid, 30 over chopper, but if you have a motorcycle or car that would make the trip, do it. You will thank me later.

We had our first legitimate gas scare as all three of us had switched to reserve and were running on fumes in the middle of nowhere. Then, like some desert mirage, we hit a junction that had a gas station.

As we hit the second to last gas stop that day, you could literally fry an egg on any part of our motorcycles. The sun was setting, ensuring that we would have around 120 miles to do in the pitch black. So considering what we had been through the night before, Dalen and I repacked our bikes so our lights weren't blocked and I had to wear a 50-pound backpack the whole way into Indio. Naturally, that added much more pressure to a wound that was bleeding through three layers of fabric. We headed out of that gas station with one goal: make it to Indio alive and jump in my dad's pool when we got there.

"I THINK THAT IF GOD RODE A BIKE, HE'D RIDE A HARLEY-DAVIDSON CHOPPER."

—INDIAN LARRY

There is a magical thing that happens to an old motorcycle when it knows its about to get a rest. Riding over 500 miles in 100-degree heat had the bikes so angry that they were literally burning up from the inside out. But when the sun goes down and you're a single gas stop away from home, they start to purr. The motor hits a frequency that gets in your bones and nothing is going to prevent that horse from getting to the stable. As we ripped through the San Bernardino Mountains, down into the lowlands of Palm Desert, the landmarks began to look familiar to me. For the first time in three days, I knew I was less than 30 minutes from our sanctuary.

The remaining miles were trouble free, and as we pulled up to the gate in front of my dad's little slice of heaven, the bikes were panting in unison, knowing that the hardest part of the journey was over. We fucking made it. Over 1,500 miles in three days on a bike that most people think shouldn't go farther than from the trailer to the bike show podium.

Riding this bike, which I had spent hundreds of hours putting together, into the greatest custom bike show on earth and leaving with the Best Chopper Award from Born Free was my proudest moment to date. It sure was nice to ride home to Seattle with that aluminum plaque strapped to the front of the handlebars.

OPPOSITE: Chris tuning up his Panhead before headin' out. BELOW: Shawn jammin' on his Generator Shovel.

ABOVE: This is what freedom looks like. OPPOSITE: Snake sleeps next to his faithful Panhead in the desert.

By the end of summer, that bike had traveled almost 6,000 miles, spanning eight states and two countries, winning the Best Chopper Award at Born Free 7 and at the Spit and Shine Show up in Canada.

This chopper has gone through a transformation from show bike to survivor in one single summer. Most people can't tell if it's a survivor or not, which aligns itself a little better with the aesthetic of most of my other builds, so I couldn't be happier. It was the culmination of all these things that caused my buddies to name the bike for me. They figured The Contradiction (or Connie for short) was the most appropriate name because I always made fun of guys who do fancy paint and chrome all over their bikes, but then ended up building one myself as a way to get out of my own comfort zone.

RIDING INTO THE SUNSET

In TV and movies, when a genre has run its course and every last dime has been squeezed out of an idea, the only thing left to create is a parody. I feel that we have reached that point in the outlaw biker world. That said, the new chopper kids impress and inspire. They've redefined choppers and renewed the riding experience, giving birth to new kinds of runs and rallies. They don't buy into turf wars, they don't get upset if you accidentally bump into them, and they sure as hell don't want to shoot anybody. For the most part, this revolution is a peaceful one. Like Peter Fonda told us in *The Wild Angels*, "We just want to be free to ride our machines." Truer words were never spoken.

"MOTORCYCLES WERE ALL I COULD REMEMBER SINCE I WAS A KID. I TRIED TO REBEL INTO THE SKATE, SNOW, SURF SCENE, BUT THERE'S JUST NOTHIN' COOLER THAN AND MORE PUNK ROCK THAN BUILDING AND RIDING BIKES."

—ROLAND SANDS, RACER AND BUILDER

INDEX

"LIFE SHOULD NOT BE A JOURNEY TO
THE GRAVE WITH THE INTENTION
OF ARRIVING SAFELY IN A PRETTY
AND WELL-PRESERVED BODY, BUT
RATHER TO SKID IN BROADSIDE, IN
A CLOUD OF SMOKE, THOROUGHLY
USED UP, TOTALLY WORN OUT, AND
LOUDLY PROCLAIMING, 'WOW! WHAT
A RIDE!'"

—HUNTER S. THOMPSON